THE CRISIS
with
RUSSIA

EDITED BY NICHOLAS BURNS & JONATHON PRICE

FOREWORD BY JOSEPH S. NYE & BRENT SCOWCROFT

CONTRIBUTORS INCLUDE:

GRAHAM ALLISON, JOHN BEYRLE, STEPHEN BIEGUN, STEPHEN HADLEY,
WOLFGANG ISCHINGER, MEGHAN O'SULLIVAN, KEVIN RUDD,
LILIA SHEVTSOVA, ANGELA STENT, AND STROBE TALBOTT

The Aspen Institute
One Dupont Circle, N.W.
Suite 700
Washington, DC 20036

Published in the United States of America in 2014 by The Aspen Institute

All rights reserved
Printed in the United States of America
ISBN: 0-89843-613-3
Wye Publication Number: 14/019

Cover design by: Steve Johnson and Jon Portman
Interior layout by: Sogand Sepassi

aspen strategy group

CO-CHAIRMEN

Joseph S. Nye, Jr.
University Distinguished Service Professor
John F. Kennedy School of Government
Harvard University

Brent Scowcroft
President
The Scowcroft Group, Inc.

DIRECTOR

Nicholas Burns
Professor of the Practice of Diplomacy
and International Politics
John F. Kennedy School of Government
Harvard University

DEPUTY DIRECTOR

Jonathon Price
Deputy Director
Aspen Strategy Group

ASSOCIATE DIRECTOR

Jennifer Jun
Associate Director
Aspen Strategy Group

ASPEN INSTITUTE PRESIDENT

Walter Isaacson
President and CEO
The Aspen Institute

MEMBERS

Madeleine Albright
Chair
Albright Stonebridge Group

Graham Allison
Director, Belfer Center for Science
and International Affairs
John F. Kennedy School of Government
Harvard University

Zoë Baird
President
Markle Foundation

Samuel R. Berger
Chair
Albright Stonebridge Group

Stephen Biegun
Vice President
Ford Motor Company

Robert D. Blackwill
Henry A. Kissinger Senior Fellow for
U.S. Foreign Policy
Council on Foreign Relations

Kurt Campbell
Chairman and CEO
The Asia Group, LLC

James Cartwright
Harold Brown Chair in Defense Policy Studies
Center for Strategic & International Studies

Eliot Cohen
Adjunct Senior Fellow
Center for a New American Security

Acknowledgements

Nicholas Burns
Director, Aspen Strategy Group

Jonathon Price
Deputy Director, Aspen Strategy Group

As with all the work of the Aspen Strategy Group, the volume you hold today would not be possible without our supporters and partners.

We are proud that many foundations, individuals, and corporations agree with our underlying thesis: nonpartisan and open dialogue among a diverse group of individuals can bring forward new ideas and meaningful solutions to some of the major challenges the United States faces. The ASG provides a forum where experts can take time to comprehend the issues better, providing background and context to the challenges of the day while looking to find concrete policy solutions. Unfortunately, venues for this type of deep dialogue are all too rare. The Aspen Strategy Group has been working to promote and host this style of convening for 30 years.

The topic of this year's publication is familiar ground for the group: it was founded on arms control issues in 1984. And the theme of U.S. policy towards Russia has woven through the ASG's long history even as our membership and focus broadened over the decades.

Over the last 30 years, the Strategy Group has taken on the biggest issues facing America. We have examined the contours and complications of American grand strategy in the Middle East, the national security implications of petro-politics and climate change, and the dangers emanating from cyber space, among many other topics. But Russia has never been far from the group's minds, and even 30 years later the ASG and Russia remain inextricably linked.

In fact, this volume is one in a series of publications the ASG has written on Russia over the years—most recently in 1993 and 1999. As with all our books, we hope this will be of interest to students, citizens, and policy makers alike, especially those who wish to gain an insight into how the experts that influence and shape U.S. policy view the future of U.S.-Russia relations in the next 15 or 30 years.

We are grateful to the individuals and organizations who invest their time and money to bring these ideas to the Strategy Group and the wider public. We would like to extend the deepest thanks to the John Anson Kittredge Fund, the Stanton Foundation, the Markle Foundation, the U.S.-Russia Foundation, Ford Motor Company, the Resnick Family Foundation, the Margot and Thomas J. Pritzker Family Foundation, DRS Technologies, Mr. Simon Pinniger and Ms. Carolyne Roehm, Mr. Howard Cox, Mr. Robert Rosenkranz and Dr. Alexandra Munroe, Mr. Robert J. Abernethy, and Ms. Leah Joy Zell.

Of course this volume would not be possible without the invaluable contribution of distinguished Aspen Strategy Group members and outside experts who wrote these papers or offered their advice and comments to the authors. We would also like to thank our Associate Director, Jennifer Jun, and our Brent Scowcroft Award Fellows, Peter Walker Kaplan, Brandon Kist, and Agnieszka Kurzej for all their work to produce both the summer workshop and this book. They are well on their way to promising careers in foreign policy. We are grateful for the services of Gayle Bennett in proofreading and editing this publication.

Finally, we must acknowledge that the Aspen Strategy Group was just an idea, until 1984, when the "founding three": Brent Scowcroft and William Perry as Co-Chairmen and Joseph Nye as Director gave the idea life. Now, as then, they remain some of the most respected thought leaders for their extraordinary service and commitment to the Strategy Group's mission of nonpartisan dialogue. The ASG would not exist without them.

As the Strategy Group reflects on the last 30 years, we are more convinced than ever that we fulfill an important and unique role as a nonpartisan forum, where strategic thinkers from the right and left sit down together without partisan acrimony to solve America's most difficult challenges. As long as they're willing to do so, the Strategy Group will have the round table ready for the next conversation.

Contents

Foreword by ASG Co-Chairmen 11
Joseph S. Nye, Jr. and Brent Scowcroft

Preface by ASG Director 15
Nicholas Burns

Part 1

The Sixth Annual Ernest May Memorial Lecture 21
Putinism: The Backstory
Strobe Talbott

Part 2

CHAPTER 1
The World According to Putin 35
Lilia Shevtsova

CHAPTER 2
Putin's World 51
Angela Stent

CHAPTER 3
The Ukraine Crisis and Beyond: A European Perspective 63
Wolfgang Ischinger

Part 3

CHAPTER 4
Sino-Russian Relations 75
Kevin Rudd

CHAPTER 5
The Unconventional Energy Boom: Bad Timing for a Revanchist Russia 85
Meghan L. O'Sullivan

Part 4

CHAPTER 6
Advice for the Obama Administration on Putin, Russia, and Ukraine.......103
John Beyrle

CHAPTER 7
Russia and the United States' National Interest (Or Reset Version 2.0) 111
Stephen Biegun

CHAPTER 8
Russia, the Ukraine Crisis, and American National Interests.............127
Graham Allison

CHAPTER 9
Concluding Observations: What We Heard................................143
Stephen Hadley

Foreword
by ASG Co-Chairmen

Joseph S. Nye, Jr.
ASG Co-Chairman
University Distinguished Service Professor
John F. Kennedy School of Government
Harvard University

Brent Scowcroft
ASG Co-Chairman
President
The Scowcroft Group, Inc.

This volume contains the main insights and ideas from the Aspen Strategy Group's 2014 Summer Workshop discussions. Titled "Redux: Prescriptions for U.S.-Russia Policy," our 30th anniversary workshop was partially a "lead back into the past," as Strobe Talbott aptly characterized it in his Ernest May Memorial Lecture.

Given the events in Ukraine and the tensions it has wrought, America finds itself in familiar territory with the Russians. Accordingly, the ASG opted to spend this summer returning to its roots as a U.S.-Russia mediation forum.

ASG's 30-year history is inextricably tied to the arc of U.S.-Russia relations. Beginning in 1971, the late Paul Doty hosted a series of summer workshops at the Aspen Institute focused on arms control. In 1983, we worked with the Rockefeller Foundation to re-conceptualize the organization as a strategy group consisting of individuals without any university connection, who focus broadly on strategy rather than just arms control. We felt it important to recruit bipartisan chairs that were respected in both parties—Brent and William Perry were the perfect fit and Joe served as director. Following this consensus on leadership and mission, we convened ASG's first official meeting in August 1984.

We met to understand the divergences in America's relationship with the Soviet Union given the grave security threats facing the international community at the time. This endeavor, along with a rejection of partisanship, has inspired our mission since then.

In the foreword of our 1993 publication, *Securing Peace in a New Era*, the group's mission is communicated this way: "the ASG aims to relate differing perspectives about the long-term direction of international security to current policy debates in the

United States." Our commitment to the diversity of ideas and voices is unflinching, and has remained unchanged from our genesis.

We have, however, evolved in other aspects. Throughout ASG's first decade, our workshops, policy planning sessions, and track-II dialogues largely concerned U.S.-Soviet relations. However, as the years went by, the world changed, and so the Strategy Group, too, examined other challenges. Conversations on Russian arms control strategy transformed into more generalized inspections of arms control policy and its regional implications.

But Russia never strayed far from group members' minds. In 1993 and again in 1999, U.S.-Russia policy was the focus. Our publication from the 1999 meeting, *America and Russia: Memos to a President*, foresaw a turbulent future for the nascent Russian government, with many of the group's predictions playing out today in Ukraine and elsewhere.

This summer, 30 years since the ASG's founding, Russia is once again at the forefront of American policy discussions. Our 2014 meeting framed the state of U.S.-Russia relations and sought nonpartisan strategy suggestions for current and future administrations. We used the four-day workshop to examine U.S.-Russia history, Russia's internal affairs, Putin's own history and profile, the role of multilateral institutions such as NATO and the EU, the implication of the unconventional energy revolution, and Chinese-Russian relations, among others.

Our members uniformly converged on a number of conclusions. First and foremost, our members took special note of history, looking carefully at how past events have influenced the current dynamics in Ukraine. Any U.S. policymaker must not only be aware of this history, but must take it into account in developing any future strategy. Second, the group recognized that Putin's current war has an unconventional character, and, therefore, new measures, beyond expanding NATO activity, are necessary to adapt to Putin's unique warfare. Third, European, specifically and prominently German, collaboration is necessary to oppose Russian aggression. Finally, Ukraine's grim economic status worried participants, who feared that further destabilization will make Ukraine a riskier foreign aid recipient. U.S. policy must be ready to respond to all of these challenges.

Over the course of these 30 years, our meetings in Aspen have driven policy and informed opinion, reacting to and playing a role in international affairs. Despite some similarities to the heady days of the Cold War, today's Russia is a wholly different challenge—one that exists in a highly networked world of both young regimes and aging powers, challenges we've seen before and challenges we did not foresee. The papers in this book reflect on all of these changes, examining the past while offering a new collection of ideas and suggestions for the days, months, and years ahead.

Preface

Nicholas Burns
Aspen Strategy Group Director
Professor of the Practice of Diplomacy and International Politics
John F. Kennedy School of Government
Harvard University

After a generation of peace in Europe since the Cold War's end, Americans suddenly find themselves in a "back to the future" crisis with Russia. The extraordinary events of 2014—Russian President Vladimir Putin's invasion and occupation of Crimea, his subsequent campaign to destabilize eastern Ukraine, and unprecedented sanctions by the West in response—have produced the most serious crisis in Europe since the collapse of the Soviet Union nearly a quarter of a century ago.

This was the central issue discussed at the 30th annual meeting of the nonpartisan Aspen Strategy Group in Aspen, Colorado, in August 2014. Led by our co-chairs and founders, former National Security Advisor Brent Scowcroft and Harvard Professor Joseph Nye, a group of 60 current and former government officials, leading academics and journalists, and business leaders assembled for four days of intensive and often intense discussions among Republicans, Democrats, and Independents. We were joined by experts from Russia, Europe, and the Asia-Pacific region.

One of the products of the meeting is this book—a collection of the major policy papers written by leading experts on Russia's crisis with the West. Successive chapters focus on the most important questions produced by this crisis. What does Putin want? What is his strategic ambition in Europe? How should the U.S. and Europe respond? What are the long-term implications for global energy and economics, for peace in Europe, and for Russia's relations with NATO, the European Union, and China?

Our Aspen Strategy Group meetings are off-the-record so that members and guests can speak candidly. But, we started the first day with one on-the-record, public discussion before an overflow audience at the Aspen Institute's Greenwald Tent; I moderated a fascinating discussion with former Secretary of State Condoleezza Rice, former Secretary of Defense Robert Gates, and former Secretary of State Madeleine Albright. You can read the transcript or, better yet, watch the 90-minute discussion on the Aspen Institute's website: www.aspeninstitute.org/video/crisis-in-russia

As a long-time observer of the U.S.-Russia relationship, I certainly believe this is the most consequential and worrisome U.S.-Russia crisis since the end of the Soviet Empire. I was privileged to serve on the National Security Council staff at the White House from 1990 to 1995 as an advisor on Soviet affairs for President George H.W. Bush and then as a special assistant to President Clinton and senior director for Russia, Ukraine, and Eurasia affairs. I remember distinctly the collective feeling of relief and even elation in Washington when the Cold War ended peacefully, without a shot fired, after the Warsaw Pact fell and communism was defeated throughout Eastern Europe and the former Soviet Union. Those were more optimistic days; we believed a new era of peaceful and even cooperative relations might be possible with the Russian people and government.

Twenty-three years later, President Obama now faces a very different challenge. Putin's invasion of Georgia in 2008 and of Crimea and eastern Ukraine this year has suddenly produced new dividing lines in Europe. By intimidating and threatening Ukraine, Georgia, Moldova, and Armenia from even considering trade agreements with the European Union, Putin seeks to build a band of buffer states to the south and west of the Russian Federation to insulate his country from NATO and the European Union.

In response, Obama, German Chancellor Angela Merkel, and other Western leaders have now imposed on Russia tough sanctions designed to cut off investment in its energy and financial sectors. Putin's actions are also causing Europeans to look for ways to reduce their long-term dependence on Russian oil and gas imports. NATO has stiffened its defenses on the territory of its easternmost members and reaffirmed its Article V security guarantee for Estonia, Latvia, Lithuania, Poland, and other frontline states.

While it would be an exaggeration to assert that we have returned to a new Cold War with Russia, there is no doubt that Cold War-like passions have been aroused.

This book provides insights, analysis, and recommendations from some of our country's leading thinkers on how the crisis unfolded, what it means for Americans, and how we should respond. It is fair to say that the vast majority of the conference participants supported a strong and principled North American and European response opposing Russia's predatory actions. None supported going to war with Russia over this crisis. But, nearly all believed some form of sanctions and political isolation are essential.

At the same time, there was a recognition that we cannot afford to cut off all contacts with Putin and the Russian government. I certainly believe that while we must impose tough sanctions and strengthen NATO, we also have to maintain open discussions with the Russian government on the major issues where its cooperation is essential—stopping Iran from becoming a nuclear weapons power, containing North Korea's irresponsible regime, and working with Moscow on nuclear non-proliferation, terrorism, and the bloody conflicts in the Middle East.

More than a half-century ago, President Kennedy famously said that Americans would have to commit to a "long, twilight struggle" against the Soviet monolith. While this is a very different crisis, what to do about Russia will remain an abiding concern of the American people and our leaders for many years to come.

It is our hope that this book may help decipher the crisis, place it in its larger European and global context, and suggest ways by which we can defend Western interests and preserve peace in Europe for the years ahead.

Nicholas Burns is Professor of the Practice of Diplomacy and International Politics at the Harvard Kennedy School of Government. He is faculty director of the Future of Diplomacy Project and faculty chair of the programs on the Middle East and South Asia. He writes a bi-weekly foreign affairs column for the *Boston Globe*. He is a member of Secretary of State John Kerry's Foreign Affairs Policy Board at the U.S. Department of State, Director of the Aspen Strategy Group and a Senior Counselor at the Cohen Group. He served in the United States Foreign Service for twenty-seven years until his retirement in April 2008. He was Under Secretary of State for Political Affairs from 2005 to 2008. Prior to that, he was Ambassador to NATO (2001-2005), Ambassador to Greece (1997-2001), and State Department Spokesman (1995-1997). He worked on the National Security Council staff where he was Senior Director for Russia, Ukraine and Eurasia Affairs and Special Assistant to President Clinton and, before that, Director for Soviet Affairs for President George H.W. Bush. Earlier in his career, he worked at the American Consulate General in Jerusalem and in the American Embassies in Egypt and Mauritania. He serves on the Board of several corporate and non-profit organizations.

Part  I

The Sixth Annual Ernest May Memorial Lecture

Putinism: The Backstory

Strobe Talbott
President
The Brookings Institution

"In short, precisely because Putinism is, as our topic puts it, redux—that is, a conscious attempt at bringing back from the past a model for Russia's future—it's doomed."

—STROBE TALBOTT

The Sixth Annual Ernest May Memorial Lecture

Putinism: The Backstory

Strobe Talbott
President
The Brookings Institution

Editor's Note: Strobe Talbott presented the annual Ernest R. May Memorial Lecture at the Aspen Strategy Group's August 2014 workshop in Aspen, Colorado. The following are his remarks as written for delivery. The Ernest May Memorial Lecture is named for Ernest May, an international relations historian and Harvard John F. Kennedy School of Government professor, who passed away in 2009. ASG developed the lecture series to honor Professor May's celebrated lectures.

Thanks, Joe [Nye]. You, Brent [Scrowcroft], and Nick [Burns] have come up not just with a snappy tagline for our meetings over the next few days but a very appropriate one: "Redux," which is Latin for "lead back," as in "lead back into the past." That's what Russia's government is doing in two respects: it's negating and reversing the reforms of the recent past—the late 1980s and '90s—while reinstating key attributes of the preceding old regime as defining features of an atavistic new regime.

That's the essence of "Putinism." As best I can tell, the term was coined by the late Bill Safire in late 2000, nine months into Putin's first term—rather prescient on Bill's part. But the content of Putinism, the motivation and rationale for it, and the constituencies behind it, predate Putin's own appearance on the scene. Those go back to nearly 30 years ago, when he was a mid-level K.G.B. officer, attached to the Second Chief Directorate, stationed in Dresden, where his job was not espionage but counterespionage: that is, identifying, thwarting, defeating, and often destroying the enemies of the Soviet state. Back in Moscow at that time, there were powerful individuals who came to see Mikhail Gorbachev as, himself, an enemy of that state.

In looking back to the twilight of the Soviet era, let's adopt the Ernie May technique of "thinking in time": that is, by recalling what Gorbachev wanted to do—and what he thought he was doing—when he was in the Kremlin.

Gorbachev ascended to highest office in the Soviet Union 29 years ago with what he believed was an obligation to save the country. The status quo, he was convinced, was holding the U.S.S.R. back, preventing it from competing and prospering in a globalizing world. His supporters often expressed this aspiration with a deceptively modest-sounding phrase: Russia's need to become "a normal, modern country." Yet normalization and modernization required a radical break with Gorbachev's predecessors, from Lenin to Chernenko.

Take the language of reform: the vocabulary of Gorbachev's program was, tellingly, made up of two Russian words and two borrowed from English: *glasnost* and *perestroika*, *demokratizatsiya* and *partnyorstvo* with the West. These were not just descriptors of Kremlin policy—all four were antonyms of the watchwords of the Soviet internal regime and the Soviet worldview. As such, they were anathema to some of Gorbachev's supposed comrades.

In June of 1991, his own prime minister, Valentin Pavlov, mobilized an effort in the parliament to weaken Gorbachev's powers as a prelude to removing him. The proximate incitement was a plan, known as "the Grand Bargain," that Gorbachev's advisor, Grigory Yavlinsky, and our colleague, Graham Allison, had proposed as a way of garnering Western economic aid in support of *perestroika*. It's worth noting that Lt. Col. Putin's ultimate boss in the K.G.B., Vladimir Kryuchkov, was active in this cabal. He and Pavlov saw the Grand Bargain as, and I quote, "a conspiracy to sell out the motherland to foreign interests."

Senior officers in the Soviet military and security services had their own version of that complaint. They were infuriated by Gorbachev's willingness to compromise, largely on American terms, in arms-control negotiations on conventional forces in Europe, on the Zero Option for Intermediate Nuclear Forces, and, most stunningly, in Reykjavik, on Ronald Reagan's proposal to eliminate all nuclear weapons. In short, on the core issues that had led to the creation of the Aspen Strategy Group 30 years ago, in 1984, and that kept quite a few of us here today busy for decades afterward.

The so-called constitutional coup of June '91 failed, but its instigators didn't give up. The fear that Gorbachev was selling out to the West grew stronger, leading Kryuchkov and the K.G.B. to attempt a real coup two months later, which ruined

Brent's vacation (not to mention his boss's) at Kennebunkport in August '91. And, even more, it put a real damper on Gorbachev's summer holiday in Crimea.

But the putsch backfired spectacularly. It accelerated not just the terminal decline of the Soviet system, but the terminal weakening of the centripetal forces that had, for all those decades, kept the Soviet Union itself intact.

That brings us to the No. 1 terminator: Boris Yeltsin. He was a Gorbachev protégé turned rival. He was a Soviet functionary and Communist Party member who ultimately converted to an anti-Soviet, anti-Communist revolutionary.

Yeltsin was the antithesis of Pavlov and Kryuchkov. He was impatient with Gorbachev for proceeding too slowly and too timidly with perestroika, glasnost, and demokratizatsiya. In other words, Yeltsin out-Gorbacheved Gorbachev as a reformer, which made him popular with the growing number of citizens who were fed up with the system; but it also meant he out-Gorbacheved Gorbachev as a threat to the old guard. Gorbachev, seeing Yeltsin as a political liability as he tried to manage the increasingly fractious leadership, expelled him from the Politburo. Yeltsin's reply was, in effect: "You can't fire me—I quit!" He resigned from the Communist Party. But he didn't stop there. Having quit, he set about liquidating the mega-firm of U.S.S.R. Inc. and making himself the C.E.O. of its largest spinoff—an independent, democratic Russian Federation.

The dissolution of the Soviet Union was the last thing Gorbachev wanted—and it became the wedge issue that Yeltsin used to replace Gorbachev in the Kremlin, bringing down the hammer-and-sickle Soviet flag over the Kremlin and flying in its place the Russian tricolor.

But on other issues, the transition between them was—in its essence and direction—almost seamless. Those issues included how Russia should govern itself and how it should behave beyond its borders. For Yeltsin, that meant deciding where Russia's borders were. His decision was crucial to what happened in the years that followed—and what didn't happen.

That decision was to maintain the inter-republic borders of the old U.S.S.R. as the international borders of the Commonwealth of Independent States. There would be no redrawing the political map to align with the ethnographic one. Yeltsin's insistence on that point further riled his already fraught relations with the enemies he inherited from Gorbachev. For them, the most emotive bloody-flag grievance was not just the loss of territory, but the stranding of some 25 million ethnic Russians in what were now 14 neighboring states. A common phrase—mumbled, growled, and sometimes screamed—was that Yeltsin was guilty of "the mutilation of Mother Russia," leaving her orphans outside the care of Moscow.

Much as Pavlov had turned against Gorbachev, Yeltsin's own vice president, Alexander Rutskoi, turned against him. Rutskoi had a large map of the U.S.S.R. on the wall of his office. "That's the past," he liked to tell visitors, "but it's also the future." In other words, "We'll be back!" The first step, he often said, would be the recovery of Crimea. The second would be Transnistria.

This aggressive nostalgia for the past and the territory that came with it rattled Yeltsin's team, so one member decided to rattle the world. In December 1992—about the time of the post-Soviet Russia's first anniversary—Andrei Kozyrev shook up an international conference in Stockholm by impersonating whoever might be his successor as foreign minister if Yeltsin were overthrown. He played it for real, pretending to enunciate a new set of policies, two in particular: first, Russia's traditional and fated orientation was toward Asia, not Europe; second, Russia would use military force to compel other former Soviet republics, particularly Ukraine, to join a new federation with its capital in Moscow. Only at the end of Kozyrev's speech did he say it was a bit of shock treatment to bring the world's attention to a real danger.

And so it was. The following year—in October of 1993—a critical mass of Yeltsin's parliamentary opponents, whose views and intentions Kozyrev had laid out in Stockholm, exploded into violent rebellion. Rutskoi and others converted the Russian White House into an armed camp that dispatched gangs to maraud around the city, firing rocket-propelled grenades at the central TV station. Yeltsin responded with lethal force to crush the uprising.

Two months later, Yeltsin's enemies struck at him again, only this time by taking advantage of a Gorbachev reform that Yeltsin had benefited from and solidified: democratization. Russia's first post-Soviet parliamentary election produced a big win for Vladimir Zhirinovsky's ultranationalists with a strong showing by Gennady Zyuganov's communists. The platform of their so-called "national-patriotic bloc," color coded brown and red, included the obligation to defend the rights of the Russians in the near-abroad. Zhirinovsky vowed to regain Russia's lost lands in Turkey, Finland, and—I'm not making this up—Alaska.

Point being: irredentism was, throughout the '90s, at the core of the anti-Yeltsin opposition. Yeltsin's stubborn refusal to countenance irredentism—his affirmation of the existing inter-republic borders—made possible the relatively amicable and orderly self-dismemberment of the U.S.S.R. It also facilitated the creation of the Partnership for Peace as well as other institutional arrangements that were meant to bring C.I.S. members, including Russia, plus the Baltic states, into an inclusive, integrated, post-Cold War, pan-European—to some degree even pan-Eurasian—security structure.

It's important that we remember—and that we remind the Russians—that the integration of the C.I.S. into inclusive post-Cold War international structures wasn't just a Western demand or aspiration that was imposed on the post-Soviet leaders. It was an aspiration of their own that we in the West responded to and supported.

Since Ernie May had a cautious respect for counterfactuals, let me pose one here. Had Yeltsin and his fellow post-Soviet leaders set off an irredentist free-for-all in the post-Soviet space, stretching across 11 times zones with tens of thousands of nuclear weapons in the mix, it would have been a world-threatening catastrophe. On a more specific and less apocalyptic level, it would have been impossible to persuade Ukraine to turn over its Soviet-era nuclear arsenal to Russia, especially if Yeltsin's opponents had succeeded in their demand that Ukraine turn over Crimea as well.

Throughout the '90s, the world had in Yugoslavia an ongoing reminder of the fate that the U.S.S.R. avoided. That was the good news.

Here's the bad news. Russia's—and Yeltsin's—relations with the West were still stressed almost to the breaking point by the mayhem in the Balkans, particularly during its Kosovo phase in 1999. That was for multiple reasons: NATO went to war for the first time; it did so in disregard of Russia's opposition; its principal target was the capital of a nation with a Slavic Orthodox majority and, therefore, with strong historical and cultural ties to Russia; and the operation's beneficiaries were Muslim secessionists inside Serbia. That led many Russians at the time to analogize Kosovo to Chechnya. They felt they were impotent bystanders watching a preview of what NATO would someday do to dismember Russia itself. And on top of all that, at the height of the crisis, Yeltsin was in decline, physically and politically, and already pondering his own retirement.

Put that all together, and it was something of a miracle—not to mention a prodigy of political courage—that despite the flak he was taking at home, Yeltsin helped bring the war to an end on NATO's terms. He did so by investing Viktor Chernomyrdin with plenipotentiary powers to convince Slobodan Milosevic that Russia was not going to save him from a NATO invasion. Chernomyrdin also agreed that Russian forces would participate, under NATO, in an international peace-keeping force in Kosovo. That was, from our standpoint, a vital condition to assure unity of command.

From the other side of the looking glass, however, the Russian military saw it as yet another galling, humiliating capitulation to the West. Some of the top brass in Moscow held out against the arrangement throughout the many weeks of negotiations. Their agent within Chernomyrdin's "team" (and I use that term loosely) was a three-star general named Leonid Ivashov. Ivashov insisted that the Russian peacekeeping force in Kosovo must be independent of NATO and have responsibility for its own "sector," which would have become a haven for diehard Serbs, who, under Russian protection, could then destabilize the rest of Kosovo and create the conditions for Russia and NATO to themselves come into conflict. Chernomyrdin repeatedly overruled Ivashov's efforts to thwart an agreement. But Ivashov didn't give up. That was because some of his superiors in Moscow were not giving up.

The result was an episode that a number of us here remember vividly: Toria [Nuland], Madeleine [Albright], Sandy [Berger], Jim [Steinberg], as well as Javier [Solana] and Wolfgang [Ischinger], who were crucial European colleagues throughout the '90s. I'm zeroing in on this one incident not because we've got a quorum for a reunion but because it was the moment when Vladimir Putin became a visible figure in the backstory of the "ism" that now bears his name.

In June 1999, a ceasefire was in effect on the ground and in the air over Serbia. Toria and I were in Moscow with an interagency delegation to put the finishing touches on the arrangement Chernomyrdin had endorsed. While we were there, it became clear that the deal was coming undone. Our uniformed Pentagon representatives— Generals Doc Foglesong and George Casey—met with Ivashov, who reasserted the demand for an independent Russian sector, adding the threat that if NATO didn't back down on this point, Russia would establish one unilaterally. Meanwhile, a Russian armored unit attached to the international peacekeeping force in Bosnia suddenly pulled up stakes and set off on a mad dash eastward, presumably toward Kosovo.

I asked for an urgent meeting with Yeltsin. I was told he was "indisposed." We knew what that meant. We settled for a meeting with his national security advisor, Putin. It was, at the time, a creepy encounter—and all the more so in retrospect. His manner was superficially cool, professional, and courteous, but iciness and controlled contempt were just under the surface. What really struck us was the aplomb, smugness, and brazenness with which he lied.

It was spectacular—and, I'd add, reckless. Although he had to know exactly what the military was up to, he assured us that the terms Chernomyrdin had agreed to were still valid and "nothing untoward" (that's a quote) would happen to upset the hard-won peace and the U.S.-Russian deal that made it possible. Then—gratuitously and implausibly—he told us that he'd never even heard of "this Ivashov." That was like Sandy Berger saying he'd never heard of George Casey at a critical moment of high-stakes diplomacy in which George was a key participant.

Within hours, the Russian unit of about 250 troops was setting up a base camp at the Priština airport. Our own delegation set up a kind of base camp of our own in the Defense Ministry on Arbatskaya Square, where we pulled an all-nighter trying to defuse the crisis. While the talks were tough, they were nothing compared to the knock-down, drag-out shouting match that we witnessed among the Russians. On one side were the defense minister, Marshal Igor Sergeyev, and the foreign minister, Igor Ivanov. Squared off against them was the chief of the general staff, Anatoly Kvashnin, who was clearly behind the Priština end-run, and who had been backing Ivashov's obstructionism of the Chernomyrdin mission. To make a long, bizarre, and suspenseful story short, Sergeyev ultimately prevailed over Kvashnin—but just barely, and not until Yeltsin re-emerged from his indisposition to put the original deal back in place.

Back to Putin's apparent role: in his capacity as presidential national security advisor, Sandy's Kremlin counterpart, Putin was either hedging his bets on how Russia's own interagency dynamics would play out, or he was actively throwing in his lot with Kvashnin and Ivashov—who, in turn, were defying their minister and superior officer, Sergeyev, not to mention their commander-in-chief, Yeltsin himself.

Eight weeks later, Yeltsin stunned the world by promoting Putin to prime minister and designated successor, thus setting him up to be Bill Clinton's Kremlin counterpart. During the interregnum, Putin did everything he could to burnish his law-and-order image, including identifying himself with Moscow's scorched earth conduct of the war in Chechnya ("Russia's Kosovo," as we kept hearing).

However, with regard to relations with the outside world, Putin stuck with the soothing partnyorstvo line. I saw him just before Christmas, nine days before Yeltsin resigned. Russia, Putin said, "belongs in the West." He wanted to show, and I quote, "our own people and the world that on the really big issues, we're on the same side," and he added that he had "no use" for those in his country who thought—again, his words—"isolation, retrenchment, and confrontation were an option for Russia." While he made no reference to Yeltsin, at least he was affirming Yeltsin's basic orientation. That was, no doubt, the message he wanted me to pass to Washington. While I did so, I remembered that this was the same guy who had assured our delegation a few months before that there was nothing to the reports we were hearing about the Russian army breaking bad over Kosovo.

So that's the backstory.

Here we are 15 years later, living through the unfolding big story in which Putin is the protagonist and, to an increasing degree, our antagonist. He has made himself—particularly in his third term—the champion of precisely those in his country who have for a quarter of a century favored retrenchment in its domestic order. He's rolled back democratization and enfranchisement of the regions. He's muzzled and monopolized the media on behalf of propaganda and disinformation. He's come up with his own highly revised vocabulary for what are essentially reinstatements of the pillars of Soviet rule: "managed democracy" and "the vertical of power."

In foreign policy, he's replaced partnership with competition. He's scorned Russia's European vocation and embraced the Eurasian option. He's been at it for a long time. Putin's bracing speech at the Munich Security Conference in 2007 echoed Pavlov and Kryuchkov's accusations in 1991 that Gorbachev was letting foreigners (like you, Graham) foist their interests, rules, and values on Russia.

Flash forward to this past March. In asserting the right to annex other territories inhabited by ethnic Russians, Putin gave a speech to the Duma that channeled from the past Yeltsin's enemies, Rutskoi and Zhirinovsky, in the mid-90s. Putin gave his own version of Kozyrev's "April Fool's" speech of 22 years ago—only Putin isn't fooling.

As for glasnost, it has given way to disinformation of the sort used to avoid culpability for the downing of Malaysian Airlines Flight 17: a Big Lie worthy of Mikhail Suslov, the Cold War Politburo member in charge of agitprop.

And speaking of names from the past: on ascending to the presidency, Putin kept General Kvashnin as chief of staff for another five years. Kvashnin's subordinate in the Priština gambit, General Ivashov, is today a member of Putin's informal brain trust and vice president of a recently formed Academy of Geopolitical Affairs. As for Yeltsin's principal tormentors, Rutskoi remains active in Russian politics. When Zyuganov celebrated his 65th birthday, Putin attended and presented him with a first Soviet edition of the *Communist Manifesto*. Zhirinovsky, while largely marginalized, has had a bit of a comeback as supporter of separatists in the eastern regions of Ukraine.

And speaking of that regional conflict, there are Russian veterans of the August '91 attempted anti-Gorbachev coup who have shown up as part—presumably in fairly senior roles—of the secessionist forces in and around Donetsk, Slavyansk, and Lukhansk.

The point here is that while Putin was a relative latecomer to the ranks of those determined to restore much of the old regime, he became their enabler. He has made it possible for them to succeed in recent years where they had failed before.

So there's been continuity in both attitudes and personalities as Putinism establishes itself. That leads to the question of how important personality itself is in history. More specifically, how decisive and transformative has Putin himself been? Does he deserve having an "-ism" named after him? The short answer, I believe, is yes.

I acknowledge that some degree of backsliding and backlash was inevitable after the tag team of Gorbachev and Yeltsin brought down the Soviet system, given how unpopular both had become at the time of their retirements and also given external developments that had angered the political elite in Russia. I'm thinking of the U.S. withdrawal from the ABM treaty in 2002, the U.S. invasion of Iraq in 2003, the second tranche of NATO enlargement in 2004, the colored revolutions in Georgia and Ukraine between 2003 and 2005, the formal independence of Kosovo in 2008, and, in 2012, the Magnitsky Act and NATO's overthrow of the Gaddafi regime in Libya. Those and other episodes would have complicated U.S.-Russian relations no matter who was in the Kremlin.

But since we're thinking in time, let's remember that the U.S.-Russian relationship has stayed on a positive course despite serious turbulence in the past. The trust between Gorbachev and Reagan survived the Strategic Defense Initiative. Gorbachev and Bush 41 weathered the strains of the first Gulf War. And the Bill-Boris bond held through the first tranche of NATO enlargement and the Kosovo air war.

In those cases, the state-to-state relationship was highly personalized, in large measure because of a deep-seated feature of Russian political culture. No matter who's in the Kremlin—whether czar, general secretary, or president—he wields immense personal power, not just bureaucratic power, over what Dick Pipes called a patrimonial state. There has always been a vertical of power. Whoever is at the top is hard to stop, and hard to remove. Therefore, succession in leadership is also of special importance.

So let's recap. The sequence of Kremlin leaders over the last quarter century is an extraordinary story itself, packed with melodrama, irony, suspense, farce, and plot twists—and, of course, tragedy. It's worthy of a Mussorgsky opera.

Act I opens in March 1985, when the Politburo convened to choose a successor to Chernenko, which invites another counterfactual that I think Ernie would permit: if any of the four or five candidates other than Gorbachev had gotten the job, we might well today, 29 years later, still have a Soviet Union, a Warsaw Pact, and a Cold War. Once Gorbachev was in the Kremlin, he had the power to begin forcing change. He elevated Yeltsin to help him do so, then cast Yeltsin into the political wilderness.

Act II: Yeltsin fights back and replaces Gorbachev, yet adheres to the key features of Gorbachev's own reforms. Yeltsin, too, has the trump card of inhabiting the Kremlin. Despite his late-blooming democratic instincts, he was partial to the verb tsarstvovat—"to rule as czar," which he used in the first-person singular as he asserted his power, particularly against the opposition.

But then the opera turns tragic. This democratizing czar plucks this junior operative Putin out of obscurity and anoints him as his heir. He does so for an irresponsible, ignoble reason: to protect the Yeltsin family's physical and financial security.

In Act III, Putin is as good as his word on that personal commitment. But, in just about every other respect, he shreds Yeltsin's political legacy. Putin becomes, himself, the anti-Yeltsin and, by extension, the anti-Gorbachev as well, thereby earning and exploiting the support of those forces and constituencies that had tried, unsuccessfully, to thwart Putin's immediate predecessors. Moreover, Putin's policies reflect, to a degree, a widespread public mood that includes nostalgia for Russia's geopolitical heyday and disillusionment over the downside of reform.

Taking all that into account, it's understandable that many commentators believe Putinism will be with us for a long time, perhaps longer than Putin himself.

Now we're into the zone of prophecy, which Ernie May had little use for. But since others are venturing there, I'll do so myself. I'll bet against the staying power of Putinism—for two reasons.

The first is what is new about Putinism: his basing Russian statehood on ethnicity. He's used that doctrine in Ukraine to expand Russian territory. But the concept is a double-edged sword. It could shrink Russian territory. Vast parts of that country are populated by non-Russian ethnic groups. A Russian chauvinist in the Kremlin who wears a crucifix when he bares his chest may be hastening the day when the Caucasus and Central Asia will be vulnerable to jihadists to the south, including those who are already talking about a caliphate in what is now the Russian Federation.

The other reason to doubt Putinism's longevity is what's old about it. The essence of Putinism is the essence of the regime that failed in the 20th century. It failed to modernize the Russian economy. It failed to normalize society. It failed to integrate Russia into the international community as what Bob Zoellick has called, in a different context, "a responsible stakeholder."

Those cumulative failures explain why the Soviet system and Soviet state lasted only seven decades—three score and 10 years—the biblical span of a single mortal.

Moreover, that monstrosity was not, in the final analysis, killed by its external enemies like those Lt. Col. Putin hunted down in Dresden and those he still obsesses about in his paranoid imagination from the Kremlin. Rather, it died because of its own pathologies, its own unfitness for survival in the modern world. In short, precisely because Putinism is, as our topic puts it, redux—that is, a conscious attempt at bringing back from the past a model for Russia's future—it's doomed.

I'll end by putting that point more positively. Russia—thanks in no small measure to the surviving legacies of Gorbachev and Yeltsin—is not the Soviet Union. It's not monolithic. It's bigger than Putinism—much bigger. It's also, despite the retrograde policies of its current leadership, more modern and more normal. I'd submit that the prescriptive challenge for us in the coming days is to brainstorm on how to punish, isolate, and contain Putinism while maintaining engagement with Russia as a whole.

Strobe Talbott is President of the Brookings Institution and Chairman of the Secretary's Foreign Affair's Policy Board. He was Deputy Secretary of State in the Clinton administration.

Part **2**

CHAPTER 1

The World According to Putin

Lilia Shevtsova
Chair of the Program
Moscow Carnegie Center

CHAPTER 2

Putin's World

Angela Stent
Director, Center for Eurasian,
Russian and East European Studies;
Professor of Government and Foreign Service
Georgetown University

CHAPTER 3

The Ukraine Crisis and Beyond:
A European Perspective

Wolfgang Ischinger
Chairman
Munich Security Conference

"Russia has begun a process of decline that can't be stopped. The Putin Doctrine and his undeclared war in Ukraine are confirmations of the fact that the Kremlin understands that the challenges are piling up, and the resources for dealing with those challenges are dwindling."

—LILIA SHEVTSOVA

The World According to Putin

Lilia Shevtsova
Chair of the Program
Moscow Carnegie Center

By annexing Crimea and starting an undeclared war with Ukraine, Vladimir Putin has not only undermined the post-Cold War settlement, he has also demonstrated that many Western beliefs regarding Russia have turned out to be wrong. Hopefully, Putin's puncturing of the old order will have the beneficial effect of getting the ball rolling on the process of rethinking what Putin's Russia and Putin's leadership means to the world.

Putin's game: "Let's pretend!"

Putin was chosen by Yeltsin's team to preserve the status quo and strengthen the personalized power system (the Russian System). In his background, mentality, life experience, and stereotypes, he proved to be the perfect man for the job, demonstrating an ability to experiment with different versions of one-man rule. It would be a waste of time to argue whether the driving force behind Russian developments since Putin entered the Kremlin has been either his world outlook and personal agenda or the logic of the Russian System itself. Putin's views and his understanding of power have become instrumental to the survival of Russian authoritarianism. Putin's KGB experience, his suspicion of the West, the deep complexes formed in his youth, his desperate desire to succeed by traversing the murkiest corridors of power, his reliance on shady deals and the mafia-type loyalty of close friends, his disrespect for law (demonstrated during his tenure as St. Petersburg Mayor Sobchak's lieutenant), his belief in raw force as an argument, and his tenacity and acumen in pursuing his agenda—all of these hardly prepared Putin for transformative leadership. Two personal qualities had an imprint on his leadership style: his indifference to the price of his actions and his low bar for the threat barrier. In any case, caution, deliberation, willingness to be a team player, respect for the rules, and an ability to work on a strategic agenda have never been counted among Putin's personality characteristics. Besides, before he had been picked to be the guarantor of Yeltsin's family's security, he had never been a leader even among his own gang and had not been successful in his KGB career—a strong desire to compensate for these personality failures might explain his tendency to resort to macho behavior and a bullying policy.

Having unexpectedly become the Russian leader, Putin at the beginning treaded with caution, diligently acquiring the Kremlin's art of rule, which demanded that he reassert total control over the power resources—something Putin did with success. He went even further, in fact, eliminating the counterbalances within the power verticality that had existed in the post-Stalin period, which prevented total absorption of power by one team or leader (the Communist Party control over the security services was one of these balances). For the first time in Russian history, the Russian praetorians (the representatives of the special services), who had been the "gatekeepers," became rulers, which ended in their efforts to acquire total control over all areas of public and state activity.

During his first presidency, Putin worked within a paradigm we might call: "Join the West and pretend to accept its standards." At the time, the Russian elite, recognizing the West's dominant role, tried to imitate its norms and use them to pursue its own interests. From 2000-2003 Putin even toyed with the idea of joining NATO and became America's partner in the anti-terrorist coalition. He created the illusion that he was a pro-Western economic modernizer with authoritarian aspirations—an acceptable profile for the West model. Apparently, Putin was deliberating on the mechanisms of his rule, the degree of subjugation that he should use on society, and the nature of compromises he could allow with the West. He was trying to balance his provincial longing to engage with the most powerful leaders and his suspicion of the West. Vanity was not the only explanation of his "partnership" period; he was learning to use the West to pursue his own ambitions. Putin's foreign policy made it easier for the Russian elite to integrate personally into Western society while keeping Russian society closed off from the West. This policy looked ideal for a leader who was turning Russia into an "energy superpower" that functioned by cooperating with the West.

The Soviet Union survived through rejection of the West, whereas Putin's regime has experimented with glomming on to the West. The Kremlin's imitation of the Western norms and institutions helped Putin use Western resources for the regime's needs. The emergence in the West of the powerful lobby that serves the interests of the Russian rent-seeking elite has become a factor of both the Kremlin's international impact and the preservation of the Russian domestic status quo.

During his period of dating the West, Putin apparently arrived at a couple of "truths" that now guide his policy toward the West, of which he has spoken on many occasions: the West uses values as a tool of geopolitics and geo-economics; everybody in the Western world has his or her price; there is no united West, and there are therefore many vulnerable points for "Trojan horses"; Western leaders are ready to accept double standards and imitation of "normative dimension" if they see some economic reward for doing so; and the West has no courage in responding to bullying. When in 2011 and 2012 Putin and his "talking heads" (such as Foreign Affairs Minister Sergei Lavrov) began to talk about the "decay of the West," invoking Oswald Spengler, they surely believed what they were saying. The irony is that Putin viewed the U.S. reset and the German "partnership for modernization" as confirmation of Western weakness; the West's acquiescence helped the Kremlin develop its assertive attitude toward the West.

The growing self-assuredness of the Kremlin hasn't hampered its constant whining: "The West does not respect Russia," "America encircles Russia," and so on. What has been running through Putin's mind all this time? Cockiness, or his hurt feelings and distrust of outsiders? His actions and his rhetoric allow us to conclude that the Russian president might suffer from a kind of cognitive dissonance; however, gradually, unconcealed arrogance has begun to dominate in Putin's behavior, which could be a reaction to his hurt feelings during his presidency or rather a reflection of his burning thirst to retaliate for his unhappiness and failures in the early stage of his life.

Either way, the West may have achieved some tactical gains during the "partnership" period with Putin, but one should be aware of the strategic losses: the Kremlin has learned how to use the transactional relationship with the West to serve its goals and has concluded (not without reason) that it is more deft at this type of relationship and can use it for its own advantage, and the West has lost the support and sympathy of the Russian pro-Western minority, which has become openly critical of the West's policy of acquiescence.

Putin's "strategy"

As of 2004, the moment of the Ukrainian Orange Revolution, the Kremlin started to work on a new model of survival. During Putin's anti-American outburst in Munich in 2007, he gave the West a warning: I am challenging you! What forced Putin to change his behavior?

I would argue that domestic factors have always been decisive in driving the Kremlin's polices and the evolution of the Russian System. When you hear the argument that the Kremlin's assertiveness has been due to its reaction to the humiliation it felt from the West, to NATO expansion, or to America's ignoring Russian interests, this is only partly true. But even when this is true, the disrespect (real or imagined) the Russian elite (and its leader) feels from the West comes from the way it builds and justifies its personalized rule—a way that sees all different principles or norms as hostile, threatening, and aimed at undermining them.

Could Putin's policy, as detailed above, be described as a "strategy"? And if so, how can it be defined? Was his pro-Western stance during his first presidency evidence of opportunism, or was it a genuine, albeit failed, attempt to make Russia a part of the Western community? Could he return to sustainable cooperation with the West?

I understand "strategy" as a leader's ability to have a vision of his country's development based on certain standards and values, and an ability to explain his agenda to the populace and get support for it. Putin's "strategy" from the very beginning included two ideas—"Great Russia" and "strong state"—and a package of often incompatible slogans that he has been juggling. Before long, those in Russia who had expected from Putin a new strategy that would have guaranteed Russia a clear trajectory and made it a predictable international actor were disappointed. Putin's "strategy" appeared to be a combination of operational tactics aimed at securing his personal power. At some point he may have begun to associate himself with the Russian state; this is something that has happened to nearly all Russian leaders.

Putin proved to be skillful in pursuing a number of traditional 19th-century aims—great power status and an emphasis on the role of might and territory—and doing so with 21st-century tools—intelligence, commerce, and joint ventures and investments.

For Putin, strategy, means, goals, logic … *everything* is instrumental and situational and can be changed at any moment, depending on the circumstances. He has been trying to reconcile the incompatible: apprehension regarding the outside world and its influence on Russia with an understanding that some openness is necessary (at least in order to implement the regime's economic interests); the interests of the comprador Russian elite operating in the West with the interests of the isolationist elite; imperial expansion with pragmatism; and the need to use the West for survival with attempts to deter the West as an enemy. In the end, Putin has failed to reconcile the irreconcilable and has had to shift from the civilizational ambiguity of the previous two decades to a declaration of Russia's uniqueness, which means choosing hostility toward the Western civilizational paradigm.

From imitating the West to becoming anti-West

By the end of 2013, the Kremlin presented the new political outlook based on the following assumptions: the world is in crisis and the West is in terminal decline; a "polycentric system of international relations" has emerged; competition between Russia and the West "takes place on the civilizational level"; and "Western ideology is doomed." By declaring the end of liberal democracies, Putin closed the pro-Western period of Russian history beginning in 1991, which included part of his own tenure in office.

Here are the main premises of the Putin Doctrine, which has become the ideological framework for his new political regime. First, Russia is a special "state-civilization" based on a return to "traditional values" and "sealed" by traditional religions. Second, Russia is becoming the chief defender of Christianity and faith in God. Third, Russia is going to unify the post-Soviet space and become an "independent center of global development." In short, we are talking about the return to an archaic, fundamentalist autocracy, which now clearly sets itself against the liberal democracies.

Never before has Putin chastised the West, its ideology and mentality, so blatantly. Putin announced that the Euro-Atlantic countries are "renouncing their roots" and "negating moral principles." He spoke of the West's attempts "to revive a standardized model of a unipolar world." The "Euro-Atlantic countries," he continued to press home, are undermining the foundations of "human society!" Here is a hallmark example of Putin's anti-Western mantra: "Today, many nations [There is no doubt whom he has in mind—L. Sh.] are revising their moral values and ethical norms, eroding ethnic traditions and differences between peoples and cultures. Society is now required not only to recognize everyone's right to the freedom of conscience, political views, and privacy, but also to accept without question the equality of good and evil." This rhetoric means that the Kremlin has stopped pretending and has openly declared its new agenda: to turn Russia into the counterbalance to the liberal democracies.

The Ukrainian crisis did not just allow the Kremlin to put its doctrine into practice, it also enriched it with new elements. The Kremlin has used Ukraine as justification for society's military-patriotic mobilization around the regime through turning Russia into a "besieged fortress" and fine-tuning its version of an "enemy" as one that would come from inside the country and be supported by an external adversary. At the same time, the Ukrainian crisis allowed the Kremlin to test a new way of manipulating mass consciousness. First of all, it took advantage of people's respect for the country's War World II history and popular hatred of fascism to create a phantom enemy represented by the "Ukrainian fascists" and their Western protégés. The regime manipulated public consciousness through blatant lies injected into Russian people's psyche through enormous doses of media propaganda. The tactic worked, creating unprecedented public consolidation around the country's leader: 83 percent of Russia's citizens supported Putin's "wartime presidency" in May 2014.

In its quest for the new forms of popular indoctrination, the Kremlin dared to play the ethnic card for the first time. On April 17, 2014, Putin stated that "the Russian people have a very powerful genetic code. … And this genetic code of ours is probably, and in fact almost certainly, one of our main competitive advantages in today's world. … So what are our particular features? … It seems to me that the Russian person or, on a broader scale, a person of the Russian world, primarily thinks about his or her highest moral designation, some highest moral truths. This is why the Russian person, or a person of the Russian world, does not concentrate on his or her own precious personality." Moreover, Putin declared that an ability and willingness to die in public is one of the main features of the Russian genetic code: "I think only our people could have come up with the famous saying: 'Meeting your death is no fear when you have got people round you.' How come? Death is horrible, isn't it? But no, it appears it may be beautiful if it serves the people: death for one's friends, one's people or for the homeland." This is how Putin addresses the need to sacrifice one's life, which is a wartime slogan.

The Russian leader continues searching for a new justification of his right to perpetual and unrestrained rule. Putin's set of ideas resembles a stew cooked with whatever the chef could get hold of: Sovietism, nationalism, imperialism, Russian Orthodox fundamentalism, and economic liberalism(!). The Russian president easily juggles ideas borrowed from both Russian conservatives and Western right-wing ideologists. Putin likes to refer to the Russian philosopher Ivan Ilyin, an opponent of the West who considered Nazism "a healthy phenomenon" during the rise of the Nazi Germany. "Western nations cannot stand Russian uniqueness. … They seek to dismember Russia," Ilyin complained while calling for the "Russian national dictatorship." Putin has not yet talked of "national dictatorship," but he loves to complain about Western efforts to back Russia into a corner.

The Putin Doctrine demonstrates that foreign policy has become a crucial instrument in securing the existence of the Russian System. The Kremlin's foreign policy has several overlapping functions. First, it has to guarantee the building of the external environment supportive of the personalized power. Second, when the Kremlin's internal resources have started to shrink, foreign policy has to play a compensatory role, consolidating society around the regime. The fact that foreign policy has to perform the internal functions, which usually is the domain of social and economic policies, is confirmation that the Russian System has lost its equilibrium.

Today, in the practical area, the Kremlin is conducting a two-pronged foreign policy project. First, in the post-Soviet space it seeks to create an entity that resembles "the global socialist system," but without its unifying Communist ideology. This role is to be served by the Eurasian Union, with Russia, Belarus, and Kazakhstan as its nucleus and Moscow acting as its leader. Second, the Kremlin is working on developing a dual-track policy vis-à-vis its Western partners. This policy seeks to both contain the West as a normative power and a geopolitical actor and cooperate with it (but, of course, on Moscow's terms).

The Eurasian Union is a club of authoritarian states, and its main goal is to preserve the status quo and the personalized rule in each state. The member states are prepared to participate in this Kremlin project in exchange for subsidies and security guarantees (this is especially true of Armenia and Kyrgyzstan). Moreover, the prospective members do not mind blackmailing Moscow to get higher payoff for their membership. However, the Russian subsidies do not guarantee that the members of the Eurasian Union will be loyal to Moscow; they will easily betray the Kremlin as soon as new sponsors appear.

The Eurasian Union is not the Kremlin's only initiative. In 2014, Putin put forward a concept of creating a "Russian World," an idea he borrowed from the Russian nationalists. "Russian World" is supposed to consolidate ethnic Russians globally on the basis of loyalty to the Kremlin. The annexation of Crimea became the first step in implementing this initiative. Putin also expressed his commitment to helping "Novorossiya" (the New Russia), that is, Russian speakers in the southeast of Ukraine, and unleashed undeclared war in the region. The emergence of the "Russian World" idea and the Crimean annexation conjured up some alarming analogies with the Austrian Anschluss and the annexation of Sudetenland by Nazi Germany. But since the majority of people in Ukraine's southeast were not ready to reunite with Russia, the Kremlin abandoned its idea to absorb this territory—but will try to continue destabilizing the situation there, preventing Ukraine from moving toward Europe.

We are witnessing the Kremlin's attempt to juggle two contradictory projects. While the Eurasian project is an imperial idea, the "Russian World" project is an ethnocentric initiative, which may negate the Kremlin's attempts to gather other states under its wing and undermine the unity of the multiethnic Russian Federation. Even Moscow's allies—Kazakhstan and Belarus—did not support the takeover of Crimea, and understandably so: after all, both countries have sizable Russian-speaking communities. So far, the Kremlin has managed to balance these two initiatives and even rally Russian nationalists around its cause. Most nationalists who had previously opposed Putin for many years supported the Kremlin in the wake of the Russia-Ukraine conflict. But the Kremlin will not be able to exploit these two essentially opposite initiatives for long. It will have to choose the imperial idea, since only this idea will allow it to maintain control over the multiethnic Russian state.

Putin's "operational art"

True, even now Putin still tries to blur the demarcation lines, normative distinctions, and differences of interests that say that neither he nor the Russian elite want to isolate Russia and turn it into North Korea. The Kremlin continues to operate with fuzziness, and the most spectacular example of this is Putin's attempt to erase the line between war and peace, which he has demonstrated with his aggression in Ukraine: Moscow continues to behave as if Russia has a normal diplomatic relationship with Kiev at the same time that it is waging a war on Ukrainian territory without admitting it! This "fuzziness" prevents Western consolidation and allows the Kremlin to keep various exit strategies open.

The Kremlin continues to use alternative means and instruments from its traditional tool kit: co-optation of the Western elites and assertiveness in confronting the West as a normative community and geopolitical entity; negotiations and pressure; and cooperation and threats. This incompatibility broadens the field of maneuver for the Kremlin and allows Moscow—even after it declared that it views the West as a hostile civilization—to be within the West and cooperate with the Western partners, preventing Russia's further isolation and marginalization. However, the balance between these opposites has changed in favor of confrontational modality.

One more element from the survival kit: Putin has been trying to deform the existing principles and rules, undermining the understanding of principles like legality, legitimacy, law, and adherence to treaties. He makes them vague, fuzzy, and ambiguous terms and in this way creates his own postmodernity, which means situations where goals are uncertain, means are deceptive, and rhetoric can be changed at any moment to its opposite. Having created a totally de-ideologized atmosphere within Russia, Putin's Kremlin has been extending this postmodernity to the international arena, pursuing the principle: "Principles do not matter; everything is possible; nothing is certain." Creating a Hobbesian, predatory world, the Kremlin hopes, not without reason, that it can navigate it better than the West.

After kicking over the global chessboard and enjoying his simultaneous roles as Global Spoiler and Terminator, Putin is ready to continue "engagement" with the West. Indeed he is even looking forward to it, making it clear that Russia will dictate the terms and will switch to containment in areas whenever he finds it necessary. If this is impossible, Russia will defend its right to interpret existing norms. The Russian authorities do not hide their belief that the West (first of all the U.S. and Germany—the two countries that, according to the Kremlin, have to be reckoned with) has agreed to Putin's key demands during the previous "sweet" period: the West has agreed not to meddle in Russian domestic affairs and has stopped promoting democracy inside Russia (the Kremlin does not care about Western rhetoric); the West has agreed to recognize the Russian "areas of interests" in the post-Soviet space; the West is ready to continue economic cooperation with Russia; the West is willing to "accommodate" Russia on other issues; and the West is ready to engage Russia to prevent its further unpredictability on all levels. Putin looks as if he believes that President Obama owes him for getting him out of an uncomfortable situation in Syria and is really baffled at the U.S. sanctions over Ukraine, considering them proof that the U.S. doesn't understand the meaning of the word "reciprocity."

Putin and his team, accustomed to survival in the world of the Russian political jungle and normative ambivalence, often misinterpret Western behavior. They view the Western emphasis on negotiations, consensus, and readiness for agreements as symbols of weakness and "spineless" politics. They view the very way the EU and Washington adopt their decisions as confirming a lack of courage and political will. Putin himself behaves as if he is sure that he will outfox all Western leaders.

From 2013 to 2014, Putin formulated his key foreign policy "stratagems" for the future: build up the counterbalance of the West while the West is still weak and ruled by weaklings; create a "fifth column" in the West that will support Russia; strengthen the grip over the "border lands"; guarantee Russia's energy security; strengthen its "galaxy" of satellite states; and force the West to trade off its security for concessions to the Kremlin. These are the main elements of Putin's status quo formula—he stopped thinking about modernization a long time ago. Now he concentrates only on perpetuating his survival, and he is ready to subordinate all national interests to this personal goal.

Putin's undeclared war with Ukraine provides some grounds for thinking about how he pursues his foreign policy. He does not hide his intent: to keep going and preserve his power. Ukraine was an important instrument for securing this goal as well as a playground for perfecting his doctrine.

But he is not a dogmatist, and as his September "Peace Plan" for Ukraine has demonstrated, he is ready to try various scenarios to suffocate Ukraine. Chopping off another part of Ukraine? Not excluded in the future. Destabilizing its southeast? Definitely. Creating a Ukrainian Transnistria from the occupied part of Ukraine? Certainly. Making Ukraine a failed state? No doubt. Threatening other new independent states with a repeat of the Ukrainian "campaign" on their territory? Definitely. Putin is testing the waters; he will change his tactics if needed; he can back off one day in order to return later. He is analyzing the West's reaction, trying not to provoke harsh and collective action.

So far, Putin's tactics have been partly successful. The Kremlin has failed to destabilize the whole Ukrainian southeast and failed to prevent the Ukrainian presidential election. But the Kremlin has succeeded in forcing the world to silently agree with Russia's annexation of Crimea. The Kremlin has plunged the Ukrainian eastern provinces into chaos and undermined the core structures of the Ukrainian state. The Kremlin may still succeed in securing the pro-Russian forces in the new Ukrainian parliament. Did the Kremlin pay a high price? I would guess that the price Putin paid in his mind has been worth the effort: the military-patriotic mobilization he has achieved in Russia has strengthened his grip on power, which was his main goal.

Will Putin backtrack when threatened by more painful sanctions? The U.S. and the EU sanctions have started already to produce a crippling effect on the Russian economy.

Indeed, the sanctions do worry the Kremlin. Some of the sanctions are becoming if not painful, then unpleasant for Putin's close entourage. However, the Russian leader can't reject his paradigm of survival, which in the eyes of both the Russian elite and his own base would mean surrender. He knows that if he shows readiness to obey the West's demands, he will immediately be viewed as a pathetic loser by the Kremlin hyenas, who are waiting for him to make a mistake, and he will lose the support of the patriotic base of Russian society that he has recently built.

Putin will never forgive what he believes is a slap in the face, and he surely views the Western sanctions as a slap. He will try to retaliate in such a way that he undermines neither his economic cooperation with the West nor his energy policy. He can write a playbook of revenge that he could pursue in the most pervasive ways. For example, his revenge for the Magnitsky Act was to forbid foreign adoption of Russian children. Thus, one could expect a harsh crackdown on what remains of Russian civil society, which he has been holding hostage. I am not sure he will risk an attack on Western business interests (at the moment he views the business community as the Russian lobby in the West). But he will definitely continue to militarize Russia and play with the idea of nuclear blackmail.

The Kremlin has been watching the political West during the war with Ukraine, and Putin might have concluded that he could continue to raise the stakes of engagement. He sees a lack of unity among the Western states; the crisis of the EU; Germany's reluctance to get out of its accommodation mode with Moscow; the emergence of the global left-right international, which hates the U.S. and EU and is ready to support Moscow; and President Obama overburdened with other threats and eager to retrench America. This is not an environment that hinders Putin's experiments.

Meanwhile, Western analytical narratives are often of little help in trying to understand Putin's agenda. Even now I have the impression that quite a few Western experts dealing with Russia believe that if the West finds a common strategic purpose for a relationship with Russia and gets to the highest level of the Kremlin leadership, it will help put the relationship back on track. But if this is true, then why hasn't it happened yet? Why have all previous partnership agendas ended with the same result? We have to continue "the transactional approach" to our relations with Russia, insist some experts. But these relations have always been transactional. The problem is that all possible tradeoffs were made a long time ago, and now, in order to accommodate the Kremlin, the Western leaders have to surrender their core interests and norms. Still others conclude that Russian developments and foreign policy have a cyclical nature, with periods of warming and cooling, and that nothing can be done about these cycles. This kind of determinism could hardly explain the reason behind the "cycles," but it could justify attempts to return to business as usual.

Many Western observers hoped that the destruction of a Malaysian airliner over Ukraine would become "a game changer" in the West. However, we still have to see whether the political West is ready to alter its accommodative approach to both Russia and the Russian aggression against Ukraine. The Kremlin's continuing support for the separatists, the Kremlin open invasion into Ukraine in August, and Putin's consent to a September ceasefire sends the message to the world: we'll follow our path; we can't back down under threats! In short, we see the Kremlin's effort to change tactics within the same model of behavior: change without change!

What next?

Moscow's readiness to participate in peaceful negotiations with Kiev in June-July has demonstrated that it is ready to experiment with the "peace formula," but it will make sure that Putin emerges as the key peacemaker. Putin apparently hopes that the West will accept this role because it is not ready to deal with the results of irritating him. I can't exclude that at some point Putin will even express his readiness for a new "reset" with the West and the U.S. too; if a "reset" happened after the Russo-Georgian war, why can't it happen after Moscow's war with Kiev? It looks as if Putin believes that the West is ready to let bygones be bygones to pursue its pragmatic interests.

But a new thaw in the Kremlin's relations with the West in general and even close cooperation with some Western states do not mean that Putin is ready to shelve his doctrine. He will have to keep the military-patriotic mobilization, with its permanent search for enemies, alive in Russia. The problem is that he has already used the trump card—war with Ukraine. Now he will have to find new triggers for mobilization to sustain the "sugar high."

Where else could he find enemies and areas ripe for confrontation? One could only guess. Few last year considered the possibility that Crimea would be annexed or that Russia would go to war with Ukraine. Russians and Russian-speaking populations in the new independent states might be the first objects for the Kremlin's next "defense" campaign. If Putin finds that his foreign policy bullying starts to consolidate the West and forces America to return to Europe, he can instead concentrate on domestic enemies or macho posturing in the states that are believed to be in Russia's "area of interest," like Armenia. When one has a Darwinian view of the outside world, one can always find reasons for feeling humiliated as a motive for revenge. For Putin it will be a nonstop exercise with tactics. He will not produce a Grand Strategy. He will have no Great Ambitions. He will continue to pursue suicidal statecraft.

Russia has begun a process of decline that can't be stopped. The Putin Doctrine and his undeclared war in Ukraine are confirmations of the fact that the Kremlin understands that the challenges are piling up, and the resources for dealing with those challenges are dwindling. The military-patriotic mobilization has been a preemptive policy aimed at forging in Russia a militarist identity and consolidating the elite and the broader society on the basis of the "besieged fortress" before the "grapes of wrath" within the Russian population begin to grow and ripen.

Does the subservience of Kremlin foreign policy to the system mean that the West has no chance to have an impact on Russia's role and trajectory? No—this would be another simplification. Liberal democracies had some influence on the Kremlin's choice of model in the early 1990s (though the degree of this influence is debatable). Since then, however, now that the Russian System has matured, the West can't have an impact on Russia's vector and the way Russia is ruled. But the way the West solves its problems, its posturing in the world, and the character of its policies toward Russia without a doubt influence the way Russia projects itself on the international arena. One could argue that during the past two decades the West has been creating a rather benevolent external environment for the Russian System and in some cases has even triggered the Kremlin's assertiveness.

In any case, the Kremlin has been successfully responding to all policy models applied by the liberal democracies so far: containment, engagement (selective containment and selective engagement), cooperation, partnership, reset, "dual track," and Realpolitik. But the Kremlin would have problems responding to the common Western posture based on a long-term strategy subordinating tactical purposes to the civilizational vector. Easier said than done, of course.

One can rest assured that Putin cannot escape his survival paradigm before the end of his term or before he loses power (no one is betting that he will stay through 2018). By switching to his doctrine, he has accelerated a process that might have unpredictable consequences and implications for his power, for the Russian state, and for world order. So far, we can be sure that foreign policy will remain one of the Kremlin's key instruments of rule.

True, the Putin Doctrine would meet some serious constraints. Keeping the Eurasian Union afloat will demand from Russia economic resources that Moscow can hardly afford. Partnership with China is possible, but only with Russia in the role of junior partner. The recent Kremlin gas contract with Beijing has demonstrated Putin's failure to guarantee gains for Russia. The Kremlin's hopes that it could continue to divide the West, to use its European Trojan horses, to rely on Berlin's reluctance to contain Putin's assertiveness, and to depend on the lack of will in Brussels to form a common Russia strategy could prove groundless in the longer run. The Kremlin's assumption that the West's time is over is also a bad assumption for analysis. But in the nearest-term perspective, Putin still has room to maneuver, and he will be testing new tactics.

Here is Putin's short-term agenda:

1. Guarantee the domestic resources for his foreign policy (financial and military).

2. Find the balance between "hard" and "soft" power, between containment and cooperation.

3. Make sure that cooperation with the West serves the system survival agenda.

4. Find a balance between the interests of the petro state and the interests of the military-industrial complex.

5. Respond to the concerns of the comprador rent-seeking elite, which worries about isolationist trends.

6. Find ways to support the patriotic mobilization without provoking Western consolidation and new sanctions, and look for new ways to legitimize the regime.

In fact, we are dealing with the Kremlin's desperate attempts to divert Russian society's attention from the country's growing problems and to compensate for its inability to guarantee society's well-being and security. This policy is not sustainable in the longer run, and its emergence is already a sign that the system is losing its resilience. Could this policy provoke a split or fragmentation within the political and economic elite? Possibly, but only if there is deep crisis and social turmoil.

What kind of change would occur in this case? If Putin's grip on power is no longer sustainable, his cohort may try a palace coup, and the major part of the demoralized society might welcome a new savior. In a situation in which the liberal opposition is weak and discredited, and the state has been turned into the vehicle oriented to fight an enemy, the new regime could adopt an even more repressive policy and aggressive stance regarding the West.

In any case, the Russian System's decay is currently accelerating, and Russia's political caste and society do not have much time to find peaceful ways out of the current impasse before the system starts to unravel. The Russian post-Communist leaders have built a system that deliberately lacks constitutional and political means for resolving conflicts and deadlocks, and for seeking exit from the crisis. In this situation "pacted transition" between system pragmatists and the opposition appears dim. If the USSR succeeded in unraveling peacefully, the demise and unraveling of the Russian System created by Putin could have more dramatic consequences.

The key challenge for the West today is not a strong Russia, but a Russia sliding into deep decay, accompanied by growing uncertainty and unpredictability and by the desperate attempts of its ruling elite to survive at any price.

Lilia Shevtsova is Senior Associate of Carnegie Endowment for International Peace (Washington) and Moscow Carnegie Center. Dr. Shevtsova is an Associate Fellow at the Chatham House – The Royal Institute of International Affairs (London), founding chair of the Davos World Economic Forum Council on Russia's Future, member of the Boards of the Institute for Humanities (Vienna), Finnish Centre for Excellence in Russian Studies (Helsinki), Liberal Mission Foundation, and New Eurasia Foundation (Moscow); and member of the Editorial Boards of the journals *American Interest, Journal of Democracy,* and *New Eastern Europe.* In November she joined Brookings as a nonresident Senior Fellow. Dr. Shevtsova is author of several books, including *Yeltsin's Russia: Myths and Reality; Putin's Russia; Russia–Lost in Transition: The Yeltsin and Putin Legacies; Lonely Power (Why Russia Has Failed to Become the West and Why the West Is Weary of Russia); Russia: Change or Decay* (in co-authorship with Andrew Wood); and *Crisis: Russia and the West in the Time of Trouble.*

"It is more questionable whether Putin has a "grand strategy." He may be a few steps ahead of his rivals and determined to restore Russia as a global player dominating its neighborhood, but this does not amount to a well-articulated vision of where he wants Russia to be in 10 years."

—ANGELA STENT

Putin's World

Angela Stent
Director, Center for Eurasian,
Russian and East European Studies
Professor of Government and Foreign Service
Georgetown University

What is Putin's worldview?

Vladimir Putin's worldview was shaped by a number of formative experiences prior to 2000 when he became president. He had a hardscrabble childhood, growing up in a communal apartment in post-war Leningrad, which was struggling to rebuild itself after the devastation of World War II. He was not a stellar student, but an aptitude for martial arts rescued him from "hooliganism." These early years convinced him of the possibility and necessity of enduring and overcoming adversity. He is a "Survivalist in the proud Russian tradition."[1]

Following his graduation from the Law Faculty at Leningrad State University, he joined the Leningrad KGB and reached the rank of lieutenant-colonel. His key experience in the KGB came during his time in Dresden. He served as a mid-level officer for the KGB in East Germany from 1985-1990, where he said his job was "working with people and large amounts of information."[2] He entirely missed the perestroika period in the USSR, with its questioning of Communist orthodoxy and challenge to the Soviet system. For him, the Gorbachev era represents the unravelling of the Communist system and the Soviet state he supported and had vowed to defend when he joined the KGB. Moreover, when the Berlin Wall came down, he was confronted with the wrath of the citizens of Dresden as they descended on the headquarters of the East German secret police—the Stasi—demanding justice, and no one in Moscow answered his calls for help as he furiously burned classified documents. He left the GDR unemployed and humiliated. The fall of communism and collapse of the USSR had a direct, negative impact on him. Describing the end of the Soviet Union as the "greatest geopolitical catastrophe of the 20th century" is both a political and personal issue for him, and as he sees it, his mission is to restore Russia's greatness and leading role in the world.

He eventually found a position working as the deputy mayor of St. Petersburg, responsible for foreign economic contacts in the chaotic, freewheeling 1990s, the second phase of his career. He observed how Western officials and business representatives interacted with their Russian counterparts. It was his introduction to the very specific, opaque form of capitalism that arose from the ashes of the state planning system.[3] But his time in the mayor's office was cut short by a competitive election in 1996 in which his boss and sometime mentor Mayor Anatoly Sobchak lost his reelection bid. Putin was out of a job for the second time in six years. The conclusion he drew from that experience was that democratic elections were dangerous if you could not control the outcome. Hence his preference for "managed democracy."

The 1990s was also a time when Russia was internationally weak and, from his vantage point, responding to an agenda set by the West, particularly the United States, which, in his view, treated Russia as a second-rate power. Moscow, he believes, was forced to accept American and NATO actions in the Balkans—particularly Kosovo—that were inimical to Russian interests. NATO enlargement to include Poland, Hungary, and the Czech Republic in 1999 was a further blow to Russian interests—and to Russia's security. Nevertheless, despite the fact that Putin frequently claims that he saved Russia from collapse after the disastrous 1990s, one should not forget that those years were very beneficial for his career—and catapulted him into the presidency.[4]

The experiences of the 1980s and 1990s convinced Putin that Russia lost its place in the world both because of outside pressure from the West and because of internal mismanagement during the Gorbachev era. He believes that Russia must reestablish its full "sovereignty" both domestically and globally. The West, in his view, represents an obstacle to Russia's restoration as a great power.

After 14 years in power, how does Putin see the world?

Putin's current worldview harkens back to the traditional dialectical Soviet vantage point: it's Russia against the West; any Western gain is our loss and vice versa; the West is out to destroy Russia; or, as he said in his speech announcing the annexation of Crimea, "They are constantly trying to sweep us into a corner because we have an independent position, because we maintain it, and because we call things like they are and do not engage in hypocrisy."

Putin's approach to Russia's role in the world is informed by six central maxims. First, Russia must have a seat at the table on all important international decisions and must constantly insist that its interests are as legitimate as those of the West.

Second, Russia has a right to a "sphere of privileged interests" in the post-Soviet space and will do everything it can, using economic attraction and coercion, soft and hard political power, and military force to ensure that Euro-Atlantic structures move no closer to its borders.

Third, Russia represents an alternative, superior model to decadent Euro-Atlantic civilization. Putin has for some time espoused the ideas of conservative, Slavophile Russian thinkers, particularly those of Ivan Ilyin.[5] The appeal to conservative, traditional values resonates domestically and internationally, where this "Conservative International" movement is intended to appeal to Moslem countries and to a heterogeneous group of political parties of the left and right, including the Euro-skeptic European far right, many of which enthusiastically support Putin. While it may technically be correct to say that the ideological antagonism of the Cold War is gone, Russia today argues that its values and policies are different from and superior to those of the United States. Russia is depicted as the bastion for forces that oppose revolution, chaos, and liberal ideas.

Fourth, the only truly sovereign states are those that are not entangled by alliances. As Putin told his Security Council, "Any nation that is part of an alliance gives up part of its sovereignty."[6] Russia's aim is to go it alone as an independent center of power, seeking neither friends nor allies, but partners like China, with whom it can forge coalitions to check American power and resist what it views as Washington's commitment to regime change around the world, including inside Russia.

Fifth, Putin feels that his warnings to the United States about the dangers and enormous challenges of using military force to promote regime change in Iraq, Libya, and Syria have been consistently—and disastrously—ignored. While he may relish the *schadenfreude* of seeing what is happening in Iraq and Syria, he believes that Russia was betrayed by the West after it agreed to abstain on the U.N. vote on the no fly zone in Libya, and he told the Valdai International Discussion Club that Qaddafi's demise was "barbaric."[7]

The sixth and newest element of Putin's worldview has been his explicit commitment to the idea that a Russian World (*Russky Mir*) exists, one that transcends Russia's state borders, and that Russian civilization differs from Western civilization. Since the annexation of Crimea, Putin has invoked the concepts of a "divided people" and "protecting compatriots abroad." The central argument is that, since the Soviet collapse, there is a mismatch between Russia's state borders and its national or ethnic borders and that this is both a historical injustice and a threat to Russia's security, sentiments expressed by Alexander Solzhenitsyn in his later writings.[8] As far back as 1992, Sergei Karaganov, an influential foreign policy pundit, gave a speech that foresaw Russia's shadow war in Ukraine. He argued that Russian speakers living in newly independent countries such as Ukraine, Belarus, and the Baltic states would become the prime guarantors of Moscow's political and economic influence over its neighbors after the fall of the Soviet Union, predicting that Moscow might one day feel compelled to use force to protect them, and thus its interests, in the former USSR. "We must be enterprising and take them under our control, in this way establishing a powerful political enclave that will be the foundation for our political influence."[9]

Hence the commitment to protect Russians (defined very broadly as those who identify with the Russian World) wherever they feel threatened. The implications for countries with large Russian minorities—Ukraine, Kazakhstan, the Baltic states—are disturbing, and the rhetoric of the *Russky Mir* and protecting "compatriots" evokes uncomfortable historical parallels.

What is Putin's strategy to revive Russia as a great power?

Putin's strategy for reviving Russia as a great power rests on the interaction of three concentric circles. The first circle is the former Soviet space, those countries in which Russia has historically played a dominant role and which constitute its special sphere of influence and responsibility. Russia's aim is to ensure that no Euro-Atlantic structures move into the post-Soviet space and to create its own organization—the Eurasian Union—that will guarantee Russia's dominance and *droit de regard* in this region.

Unlike other countries that have historically adapted to the loss of empire, both contiguous and overseas—the Ottomans, Austro-Hungarians, British, and French, for instance—Russian history presents a different pattern. As an author recently noted, "For the Russian state, colonizing neighboring territories and subduing neighboring peoples has been a continuous process. It is, one could almost say, part of Russia's genetic makeup."[10] Over the centuries, Russia has shrunk and then expanded again to "gather in the lands" and reestablish its Eurasian empire. As Catherine the Great famously said, "I have no way to defend my borders but to extend them." Russian sense of nationhood historically developed as it was expanding territorially. Hence, national identity is inextricably linked to control over Russia's neighbors. Putin believes that he is in the tradition of those tsars and commissars who have guaranteed Russia's security by dominating its neighborhood.

The means that Russia has at its disposal to dominate its neighbors are both "soft" and "hard." Russia's soft power focuses on its use of media—very much on display in the current Ukrainian crisis—to present a narrative that is completely at odds with the Western narrative. The population in most post-Soviet states receives much of its news from the Russian state-run media, and this tool is quite effective in arguing the Russian case that the ousting of the Yanukovych government in Kyiv was instigated by the United States, the European Union, and their "special services." Russia also uses economic and energy carrots and sticks to wield its influence. Indeed, energy is basic to Russia's position in the world today in a way that it never was for the USSR. Energy is an essential tool of great power projection. And, as we see in Ukraine's hybrid war, Russia is also using hard military power to destabilize its neighbor and render it ungovernable. While it officially denies that it has troops and military hardware in eastern Ukraine, the evidence both from the Ukrainian government and from NATO tells a different story.[11]

The second circle for Putin's great power revival is the partnership with China, the BRICs, and other developing countries, which seeks to make Russia part of a rising group that will check U.S. power and increase Russia's economic and political presence globally. But the economic fundamentals suggest that Russia can at best be a junior partner and future raw materials appendage for China. Nevertheless, China and Russia constitute an important duo in the United Nations Security Council, capable of blocking U.S. and European attempts to pass resolutions on Ukraine or Syria.

The third circle is Russia's move to reestablish a presence in areas where the Soviet Union lost its influence after 1991—the Middle East, Africa, Latin America, and Southeast Asia. Russia's two major exports—energy and arms—are the chief tools at the Kremlin's disposal for expanding its international role. Russia is also investing in all of these countries and lending money to them.

Putin no longer believes that seeking better ties with the West—especially the United States—is essential to reviving Russia as a great power. In his view, he has been rebuffed and ignored by the West for too long. President Obama's description of Russia as a "regional power" and his depiction of Putin's demeanor after the Edward Snowden asylum decision—"he's got that kind of slouch, looking like the bored kid in the back of the classroom"—have fueled this sense of insult.[12] The politics of resentment are a powerful driver. Indeed, Putin believes that Russia will become a great power by distancing itself from the West. It no longer seeks to be treated as the U.S.'s equal. Being treated as an antagonist appears to be part of the Putin plan.

As Dmitri Trenin recently wrote, Russia wants to become "the go-to country for all those unhappy with U.S. global dominance."[13]

The invasion and annexation of Crimea

Since the Soviet collapse, Ukraine has been a core foreign policy interest for Moscow and remains so today. It is not a core priority for the United States or the EU, and Putin's Ukraine policy is based on this fact of life.

The decision to invade Crimea was opportunistic. Of course, the military plans must have been on the books for some time, and Russia has at various points since the early 1990s talked about reuniting with Crimea. But the trigger was Viktor Yanukovych's flight from Kyiv on February 22. Since the summer of 2013, Moscow had fought hard to prevent Yanukovych from signing an Association Agreement with the European Union. The agreement carried no promise of eventual membership—indeed the Eastern Partnership program was designed as an alternative to a membership path—but it could have altered Ukraine's economic, and eventually political, ties to Russia and made it impossible for Ukraine to join the Eurasian Union. A mixture of Russian economic sticks and carrots—including a $15 billion loan—and EU ineptness succeeded in persuading Yanukovych to reject the EU deal and align Ukraine more closely with Moscow.

Then came the "Euromaidan" protests, the violence, and U.S. and EU intervention in Kyiv.[14] When Yanukovych abruptly decamped less than 24 hours after signing an agreement with the EU's three foreign ministers to hold early elections, Moscow realized that its strategy of the past half year had failed. Ukraine would elect a pro-European government. It is possible that Putin believed that a new, pro-Western government in Kyiv would renegotiate the Black Sea fleet lease that Yanukovych had extended until 2042 and throw Russia out of Crimea, and that the proximate reason for the invasion was to secure Russia's naval base. Moreover, the interim government in Kyiv passed a law demoting the status of the Russian language, an unwise move that was soon reversed but nevertheless angered Russophone Ukrainians. The Kremlin views what happened in Kyiv on February 22 as an illegitimate coup by a "fascist junta" backed by the United States and has used this claim to legitimize the referendum and annexation of Crimea. The Sochi Olympics were over, and it was time to act.

Crimea's annexation can only be understood against a 22-year background of Russia's reluctance to accept Ukraine as an independent country, deep divisions within Ukraine over identity, and popular disgust with the corrupt politics of both "Orange" and more pro-Russian forces in Kyiv. And it was also domestically motivated. After the shock of the 2011 Moscow anti-Putin demonstrations, the Euromaidan explosion raised the specter of another color revolution that might cross over the Russian border. Putin must have sensed that invading and annexing Crimea would be supported domestically, and not only by nationalist groups. The annexation has raised his popularity to dizzying heights, even among some of the educated urban elite. It was indeed a shrewd move to shore up his position at home.

Crimea resonated with many Russians in a way that the West—and possibly even initially Putin himself—did not anticipate. It tapped into a deep well of popular resentment about the trauma of the Soviet breakup, the perceived humiliation of the 1990s, and pride that Russia was finally reasserting itself and standing up to the West. Since the mid-1990s, when Boris Yeltsin first established a commission to determine what Russia's national identity was, the question of "What does it mean to be Russian?" has remained unanswered. With Crimea, it appears to have been answered in a way that appeals to traditional Russian nationalism but also carries dangers in that, by focusing on ethnic Russians, it risks alienating Russia's many ethnic minorities, especially those in the restive North Caucasus.

Does Putin have a grand strategy?

Putin appears to be a master tactician. Certainly, since the beginning of the Ukraine crisis, he has always been several steps ahead of the West and has set an agenda to which the West has had to respond. Although Western sanctions will hurt the Russian economy, Russia continues to consolidate its hold in southeastern Ukraine as the area evolves into another frozen conflict in the post-Soviet space.

The September 2013 proposal to jointly disarm Syria of its chemical weapons is another example of masterful tactics. President Obama, having previously announced that possession and use of chemical weapons was a "red line," was unwilling to take military action against Syria. Russia then seized the initiative, recycling a proposal that the United States had previously made. As a result, Putin appeared on the world stage as the wise statesman creating a negotiating structure that avoided military conflict and ensured that Assad was part of the negotiation team, ultimately shoring up his position.

Another aspect of Putin's tactical prowess that has been on display in Ukraine is his ability to generate and operate in grey zones, challenging the West's interpretation of facts, constantly keeping the West guessing about his next move, and undermining Western confidence by abandoning the accepted rules of the game that have prevailed in Eurasia since 1992. He has created a new reality on the European continent that has thrown Western officials off-balance.

It is more questionable whether Putin has a "grand strategy." He may be a few steps ahead of his rivals and determined to restore Russia as a global player dominating its neighborhood, but this does not amount to a well-articulated vision of where he wants Russia to be in 10 years.

What are Putin's ambitions for Russia in the long run?

Putin's ambitions are restoring Russia's domination in the post-Soviet space, containing the West and keeping it far from Russia's borders, restoring Russia as both a regional and a global power, and cementing a partnership with China that enables Russia to exercise influence internationally to a degree belied by its real economic strength.

Historically, the Russian empire and the USSR were able to project influence as regional and global powers because of their military strength, not because of their economic might. Today's Russia is in the same position. Despite his early professions about wanting to modernize Russia, Putin has limited modernization for many of the same reasons as his 20th and 19th century predecessors: the reforms needed to create a modern state with transparent institutions and effective governance and move Russia away from being a raw-materials exporter threaten vested interests and the political status quo that helps maintain the elite in power. Today's *siloviki* and their allies have done very well by accumulating the rents from energy exports in an opaque system where informal rules and structures prevail. There is no incentive—indeed there are considerable disincentives—to undertake real modernizing reforms that would diversify the economy and undermine the system.

The current Russian political elite appears to be divided into three factions, two of which favor current assertive Russian policies and one of which is more skeptical. The first group is the nationalist enthusiasts nostalgic for the Soviet era, who would like Russia to be more isolated internationally and engaged in a bitter struggle with the West. These are the people in Putin's inner circle who would like *Novorossiya* (the term they use to describe the southeast part of Ukraine) to become part of Russia again, irrespective of the economic and international costs. They are said to include his economic advisor, Sergei Glaziev, who would like the Russian economy to be more state-controlled and autarkic and less integrated with the European and world economies. The second group supported the annexation of Crimea and a tougher line toward the West but would like to see the conflict in eastern Ukraine wind down and do not want Russia to be isolated.

The third group is the economic modernizers, who are dismayed by the war in Ukraine and Russia's growing international isolation. As Alexei Kudrin, the former finance minister, said, "We have once again become the enemy of the West," lamenting the recent turn of events. He went on to say that, unlike the politicians, "Business wants to work, to invest, to build factories, to trade. And business is very worried by what it hears on radio and television."[15] Putin apparently used to listen to all three groups. It is questionable if he has much time now for the economic modernizers.

Ultimately Putin will not be able to achieve his ambitions for Russia if the country does not modernize. It faces a number of serious challenges: massive capital flight; a growing brain drain; a deteriorating demographic situation in which mortality rates among young men 18-30 are similar to those in Haiti; and crumbling infrastructure and lack of investment in human capital. It also faces a continuing low-level insurgency in the North Caucasus. History shows that Russia has the capacity to survive extreme adversity and to regroup following defeat. But this is not a recipe for achieving an ambitious global agenda. Russia can certainly act as a spoiler and thwart Western interests, but its economic fundamentals are not those of a rising state.

As long as the Putin system prevails—and it could well outlast his time in the Kremlin—Russia will continue to exercise regional and global influence because of its strategic location, its nuclear arsenal, its veto on the U.N. Security Council, and its energy resources. But its global ambitions will be checked by its economic limitations and by a leadership more concerned with righting past wrongs inflicted on them than pursuing a vision for the future. As Stephen Hadley has observed, "Rather than importing the past into the present, Russia needs to get to the point where it imports the future into the present. Otherwise it will remain a prisoner of the past."[16]

Angela Stent is Director of the Center for Eurasian, Russian and East European Studies and Professor of Government and Foreign Service at Georgetown University. She is also a Senior Fellow (non-resident) at the Brookings Institution and co-chairs its Hewett Forum on Post-Soviet Affairs. From 2004 to 2006 she served as National Intelligence Officer for Russia and Eurasia at the National Intelligence Council. From 1999 to 2001, she served in the Office of Policy Planning at the U.S. Department of State. Dr. Stent's academic work focuses on the triangular political and economic relationship between the United States, Russia, and Europe. Her publications include: *Russia and Germany Reborn: Unification, The Soviet Collapse and The New Europe* (Princeton University Press, 1999); and *From Embargo to Ostpolitik: The Political Economy of West German-Soviet Relations, 1955-1980* (Cambridge University Press, 1981). Her latest book is *The Limits of Partnership: US-Russian Relations in the Twenty-First Century* (Princeton University Press, 2014). She is a member of the Senior advisory panel for NATO's Supreme Allied Commander in Europe. She is a member of the Council on Foreign Relations. She is a contributing editor to *Survival* and is on the editorial boards of the *Journal of Cold War Studies, World Policy Journal, Internationale Politik* and *Mirovaia Ekonomika i Mezhdunarodnie Otnosheniie*. She serves on the board of the Eurasia Foundation and Supporters of Civil Society in Russia. Dr. Stent received a B.A. from Cambridge University, an M.Sc. from the London School of Economics and Political Science, and an M.A. and Ph.D. from Harvard University.

[1] Hill, Fiona, and Clifford D. Gaddy. 2013. *Mr. Putin, Operative in the Kremlin.* Washington, DC: The Brookings Institution Press.

[2] Putin, Vladimir. 2000. *First Person.* New York: Public Affairs. Chapter 5.

[3] Ed. Reed, Joyce Lasky, and Blair Ruble. 2010. *St. Petersburg 1993-2003: The Dynamic Decade.* Washington, DC: The St. Petersburg Conservancy.

[4] Hill, Fiona, and Clifford D. Gaddy. 2013. *Mr. Putin, Operative in the Kremlin.* Washington, DC: The Brookings Institution Press. Chapter 5.

[5] Robinson, Paul. March 28, 2012. "Putin's Philosophy." *The American Conservative.* www.theamerican conservative.com/articles/putins-philosophy.

[6] Putin, Vladimir, opening remarks of Russian Security Council Meeting, July 22, 2014. eng.kremlin.ru/transcripts/22714.

[7] Stent, Angela. 2014. *The Limits of Partnership: US-Russian Relations in the Twenty-First Century.* Princeton, NJ: Princeton University Press. p. 248-249.

[8] Remnick, David. March 17, 2014. "Putin's Pique." *The New Yorker.* www.newyorker.com/magazine/2014/03/17/putins-pique.

[9] Karaganov, Sergei. April 1, 2014. "The Man Behind Putin's Pugnacity." *Russia in Global Affairs.* eng.globalaffairs.ru/book/The-man-behind-Putins-pugnacity—16532.

[10] Van Herpen, Marcel H. 2014. *Putin's Wars: The Rise of Russia's New Imperialism.* Lanham, Md: Rowman and Littlefield. p. 2

[11] BBC News Europe. September 24, 2014. "Ukraine Crisis: Nato Sees 'Significant' Russian Troop Pullback." www.bbc.com/news/world-europe-29342463.

[12] Stent, Angela. 2014. *The Limits of Partnership: US-Russian Relations in the Twenty-First Century.* Princeton, NJ: Princeton University Press. p. 270.

[13] Trenin, Dmitri. July 2014. *The Ukraine Crisis and the Resumption of Great Power Rivalry.* Moscow: Carnegie Moscow Center.

[14] This refers to the anti-Yanukovych, pro-EU demonstrations that took place in Kyiv's main Maidan square.

[15] Kudrin, Aleksei, "We have again become the West's enemy." Interview with ITAR-TASS, July 22, 2014.

[16] Stent, Angela. 2014. *The Limits of Partnership: US-Russian Relations in the Twenty-First Century.* Princeton, NJ: Princeton University Press. p. 274.

"But at some point, hopefully sooner rather than later, we will have to start anew the discussion about the creation of a more sustainable, more resilient, more crisis-resistant, and more comprehensive European security architecture. Not as a reward to Putin for challenging the architecture, but out of recognition that it needs to be adjusted to new realities."

—WOLFGANG ISCHINGER

The Ukraine Crisis and Beyond:
A European Perspective

Wolfgang Ischinger
Chairman
Munich Security Conference

What started as a domestic political crisis in Ukraine has escalated into a major crisis of European security. In fact, the—almost—unthinkable has happened: there is now a war in Europe, with airplanes being shot down almost routinely and rising numbers of casualties. The risks of further escalation and miscalculation represent the gravest danger to European security in more than two decades.

In late May, I asked Ukrainian Prime Minister Yatsenyuk what the most important thing was that the West could do to help Ukraine. Without hesitation he replied: "Just stay united. That's my only request." Indeed, only by showing a united front will Americans and Europeans be able to successfully deal with this crisis. While the European Union lacks the military and political strength to face Russia alone, the United States' influence can be significantly enhanced by the economic leverage of the EU.

This crisis is not "just" about Ukraine—as cruel as it has been for the many victims and refugees in Ukraine and for the nearly 300 innocent civilians on flight MH17. Rather, the West is now facing a Russia no longer bound, apparently, by the consensus on European security established by the CSCE Final Act, the 1990 Charter of Paris, and subsequent agreements. In fact, the best label for Russia's new foreign policy is "revisionist." Thus, the crisis has far-reaching implications for Europe and for global security. Ukraine has become a battleground for the principles on which the international order of the 21st century will rest.

But is this reflected in the political, economic, and military measures Western countries have taken so far? And, besides these short-term measures, have we adequately considered the medium- and long-term strategic consequences?

What's at stake and what we must expect Russia to do

Russia carries significant responsibility for the deterioration of the situation in eastern Ukraine. If there is now a war going on in the heart of Europe, it is because Russia has done little or nothing to stop cross-border movement of men and military resources. Moscow is thus undermining the normative framework of European security that has made the European continent a comparatively peaceful region for the past few decades. The assumption held for a long time by many in Western Europe that the members of NATO and the EU no longer face any threats to their territorial integrity has been proven wrong indeed. With the annexation of Crimea, the continuing covert intervention in eastern Ukraine, and the pronouncement of a "Putin Doctrine" reserving the right for Moscow to intervene to protect Russian-speaking populations abroad (based on Moscow's estimation whether, when, and how they need protection), Moscow has unilaterally returned the history of European security to an earlier, more adversarial chapter.

To end this crisis, at the very minimum, the Russian government must stop its support for the separatists, stop the delivery of weapons and transport of fighters to eastern Ukraine, and confirm its respect of the Ukrainians' right to determine their own future. As long as these minimum requirements remain unfulfilled, Western pressure should be maintained or even increased. And the annexation of Crimea must not be allowed to drop off the East-West agenda.

A permanent solution to the crisis will require face-saving measures on all sides. This will take time. That is why it has been the right move to aim for a cease-fire agreement as a first step of crisis diplomacy. Afterward, work could begin on a comprehensive solution, the core elements of which are quite obvious: respect for Ukrainian sovereignty by all, including Moscow, affirmation of the current Ukrainian legislation concerning NATO, decentralization/autonomy for the regions, consideration of the close Ukrainian-Russian ties during the implementation of the EU Association Agreement, and a compromise and an end to the dispute over gas prices and transit. The best instrument to tackle such a comprehensive settlement package would be an upgraded Contact Group, building on the group that negotiated the Minsk agreement, including the EU, Russia, and the U.S., under the umbrella of OSCE.

Independently, Ukraine will have to tackle a comprehensive program of national dialogue and reconciliation as well as far-reaching reforms, with international and EU support, to get on solid economic footing and to extinguish corruption. All this will take a long time. And it will cost a lot of money.

Political measures

After the annexation of Crimea and Putin's refusal to honor and respect the sovereignty of Ukraine, Russia can no longer be defined as a "strategic partner." Concerning NATO-Russia relations, this means that the Alliance did the right thing by cancelling practical cooperation with Russia on joint projects, while maintaining political consultation and communication via the NATO-Russia Council. For the time being, practical cooperation on projects such as ballistic missile defense is unrealistic (and had already come to a de facto halt anyway); and while discussions within the framework of the NATO-Russia Council (NRC) may not lead to much at the moment, it is important to keep this forum in place and ready to play a useful role again in the future. NATO has learned a lesson from suspending the NRC in response to the Russo-Georgian War of 2008, which did nothing to alleviate the conflict but took away an instrument that might have helped to better deal with the aftermath of that crisis. After all, it was created precisely as a forum for discussing critical issues between NATO and the Russian Federation.

Likewise, American and European leaders should not have cancelled the G8 Summit. Rather, they should have told Russia that there was going to be only one issue on the G8 agenda: Ukraine. This would have been an opportunity to confront Putin with an unambiguous and united Western front, with G7 members jointly and personally putting pressure on Putin. Instead, we have been witnessing a succession of bilateral meetings between Putin and individual Western leaders. Are we sure Putin did not succeed in exploring and exploiting existing differences between Western capitals? Of course he did.

But punitive measures aimed at Moscow are neither our first priority nor an end in itself. The central objective and first priority of our strategy should not be to punish Russia, but to strengthen Ukraine (as well as those other countries that are now in the "twilight zone" between the European Union/NATO and the Russian Federation, such as Moldova or Georgia). Making sure that these countries, which do not have short-term prospects for membership in the EU and/or NATO, will be able to freely choose their future is a major strategic task for the West. And it is about time that we treat it as such. The best response to Putin's policy of undermining the stability and integrity of Ukraine is to support Ukraine's development into a democratic, stable society governed by the rule of law. Clearly, this will be expensive, and it will take time. But it's the best investment we can make in the future of a Europe whole and free.

Military measures

It has often been said that there is no military solution to the crisis in Ukraine. Actually, and more precisely, Russia has achieved its short-term objectives in Ukraine by applying military force. And Russia has so far not shown any serious willingness to restrain its meddling on Ukrainian territory. As a consequence, the Ukrainian army cannot be expected to and will not win this war on its own territory anytime soon. That is why the ceasefire arrangement reached in Minsk in early September of 2014 is an important first step to end the conflict. But if there is no follow-through in terms of a political settlement, a cease-fire eventually only serves to perpetuate the control of significant parts of eastern Ukrainian territory by the Russian-sponsored separatists.

The West could, in this situation, decide to upgrade its support to the Ukrainian armed forces. Indeed, Western powers could do more to help rebuild the weak Ukrainian army by supplying it, for example, with modern communication systems, armor, logistics, and intelligence support. As Ian Kearns rightly pointed out, the U.S., the UK, and France have a special responsibility because they all signed the so-called Budapest Memorandum in 1994, which offered Ukraine security assurances while Kiev agreed to give up its nuclear weapons. But there is no reason why Germany and other EU/NATO countries should not also participate.

While all 28 allies contribute to NATO reassurance, their contributions come in very different forms. Poland and the Baltic states, having repeatedly been the target of Russian provocations and threats and fearing a "just-below-Article 5" scenario would like NATO to ramp up support and demonstrate with "boots on the ground" that allied security is indeed indivisible. It is actually quite ironic that tactical nuclear weapons continue to be deployed in some NATO countries, including in Germany, with no useful operational military role attached to them anymore, while NATO struggled to come up with meaningful steps to reassure our new Eastern members. NATO has so far been reluctant to follow the Polish and Baltic argument that Russia's recent actions mean that NATO's commitments laid down in the NATO-Russia Act of 1997 do not apply anymore. While almost everybody in NATO agrees that Russia has indeed violated key prescriptions of this document, the majority feels that we should not renounce the NATO-Russia Act itself.

But we do not need to build new NATO bases close to the Russian border. Earlier this year, the United States made a smart decision by opting for rotating units and military exercises as the main components of its reassurance package. Europeans committed to ramped-up air policing in the Baltics. Building on these measures and approaches, the results of the September NATO Summit—especially the establishment of a rapid reaction force and the "persistent" but not "permanent" rotational presence in the East—represent a significant set of reassurance policies.

Economic measures

Many critics have felt that agreeing on and implementing the several rounds of sanctions have taken too long and have not gone far enough. In the United States, commentators have been quick to criticize measures adopted by the EU as too little too late. Berlin, especially, has been accused of protecting Germany's own narrow business interests. While it is of course true that business interests have had an impact on the positions of European governments, critics in the U.S. should try to see the whole picture.

First of all, it is easy to call for ever tougher sanctions if you represent a country whose home base does not have to fear anything from it. It is a different thing if it costs you—in terms of economic growth or jobs.

Second, the long-term impact of the European sanctions should not be underestimated. Russia has much to lose vis-a-vis the EU, a lot more than from U.S. sanctions, and the European Union has shown remarkable unity in applying its own sanctions. Unsurprisingly, this unity comes with a certain price tag, meaning that the pace and reach of sanctions does not satisfy the ambitions of all those who would have liked to see a quicker escalation of sanctions.

Third, it is wrong to believe that the German government is blocking tougher sanctions. Berlin has repeatedly made clear that political considerations would trump business interests—a position that has been accepted, while surely not welcomed, by German business leaders.

Fourth, we have to make sure that the costs of sanctions and cancelled deals are somewhat evenly distributed: burden-sharing in self-punishment, if you will. Finally, sanctions are no substitute for a political strategy. They are instruments applied to achieve certain political goals, but not an end in itself. And we must always make sure that all these decisions on sanctions and embargoes remain politically reversible. We must not allow our Russia policy to be taken hostage by the U.S. Congress, nor by European parliamentary decision makers!

Strategic outlook: European defense and a pan-European security architecture

As important as the debate about necessary short-term measures is, then, it cannot and must not replace a strategic discussion about long-term effects and consequences. There are many dimensions to this—including the establishment of a European energy union. I would like to focus on two critical strategic issues:

1. When, if not now, is the right time to take concrete steps toward European defense integration?

2. How can we strengthen Euro-Atlantic security structures? This refers to both pan-European structures and to the role of the EU and NATO in Eastern Europe.

When it comes to European defense efforts, the Ukraine crisis is as loud a wake-up call as there can be. I have some sympathy for the argument that a reduction of the U.S. presence in Europe might finally force Europeans to take their defense effort more seriously. But, I am afraid, we are still not really ready to take full responsibility ourselves. That is why we need the U.S. presence; that is why we need the U.S. to encourage us to pool and share our military capabilities much better, to spend our defense euro more wisely, and to finally get our act together on an EU foreign and a defense policy worthy of the 500 million people united in the EU. Frankly, it is scandalous how little bang for the buck we get in Europe. The defense expenditure of all the European countries together totals just under 40 percent of the U.S. expenditure, but the actual combat power makes up a tiny fraction of that of the U.S. At the same time, the EU countries have six times as many different weapons systems as the U.S. This fragmentation is irresponsible financially, in terms of capabilities, and in terms of interoperability.

The European governments are aware of the ineffective and inefficient use of their defense expenditures, and they know that cooperation and integration is the only way to address this problem. This is what Pooling and Sharing is all about. A study conducted by McKinsey for the Munich Security Conference calculated that European countries could save up to 30 percent per year—that is 13 billion euros per year—if they worked more closely together in weapons procurement. Now, it is true that defense integration raises many difficult issues, including matters of sovereignty. Jeanine Hennis-Plasschaert, the Dutch defense minister, had the right answer to such objections at the Munich Security Conference in 2013: "Should we really fear the loss of sovereignty? Or should we rather define the concept of sovereignty in a less traditional way?" In other words: What is the worth of sovereignty, traditionally understood, if an individual European state is no longer capable of action on its own? This would be meaningless sovereignty, wouldn't it?

Not everybody in the EU shares the vision of a European army. But we need a debate about it. It is worth noting that in Germany, for instance, there has been significant political support, for many years, for the vision of a European army. The leader of the Social Democrats has endorsed this objective. And the 2009 coalition treaty between Merkel's conservative party and the Free Democrats plainly stated: "The establishment of a European Army under full parliamentary control remains a long-term goal for us."

At the very least, then, defense issues need to be at or near the top of the agenda at European summits. Few EU decisions would impress Moscow—or anyone else, for that matter—more than determined action by the EU to take collective decisions and to actually develop into a meaningfully integrated defense community.

As far as the Euro-Atlantic security architecture is concerned, this crisis was a wake-up call as well. In 1996 Richard Holbrooke wrote: "If the West is to create an enduring and stable security framework for Europe, it must solve the most enduring strategic problem of Europe and integrate the nations of the former Soviet Union, especially Russia, into a stable European security system." He was right. Unfortunately, we are now back to square one and have added a lot of baggage. What we need is a *doppelstrategie* (a double-track strategy), denying Putin opportunities in Europe while pursuing a dialogue with him about cooperation in the interests of all, as difficult as that may be in current circumstances.

Right now is surely not a good moment for grand structural initiatives concerning an all-encompassing Euro-Atlantic security community. But at some point, hopefully sooner rather than later, we will have to start anew the discussion about the creation of a more sustainable, more resilient, more crisis-resistant, and more comprehensive European security architecture. Not as a reward to Putin for challenging the architecture, but out of recognition that it needs to be adjusted to new realities. Such a discussion should include confidence-building measures and arms control issues, including, for example, the future of the Treaty on Conventional Armed Forces in Europe, as well as the long overdue question of the reduction and elimination of short-range nuclear forces in Europe. A number of useful and important proposals have been elaborated in recent years by U.S.-Russian-European initiatives, such as the EASI Commission supported by the Carnegie Endowment or, more recently, by Sam Nunn's Nuclear Threat Initiative.

The objective should be to strengthen both rules and institutions, including the OSCE, and to review such projects as the 2008 Medvedev security treaty proposal. The OSCE was all but forgotten, unfortunately, until the current crisis reminded us that it is the OSCE that can monitor elections, that it is the OSCE that can send observers, and that there is a Vienna Document that allows military observer missions to be deployed. One of our longer-term objectives could be the preparation of a follow-up to the 1990 Paris summit—a well-prepared OSCE summit—to discuss and decide whether Russia and the West can or cannot jointly reaffirm the principles adopted 20 years ago, including the principle of the integrity of all OSCE member states, of the peaceful resolution of conflicts, and of the clear "no" to unilateral changes of borders.

One thing should be clear: the West should stick to its long-held position that countries should be free to choose their associations. If, by pointing to the example of Finland, some appear to suggest that Ukraine should now be permanently denied the prospect of becoming a NATO member, we should not agree because this is not what the Finnish model represents. Finland could, at any moment it chooses, apply for membership in NATO. NATO never said, and Finland—to my knowledge—never accepted that this was not an option. The Finland model should therefore not be construed as excluding any country from NATO. It is a matter for Finland to decide whether or not to take steps in the direction of NATO, and it is a matter for the Alliance to issue an invitation. As far as Ukraine is concerned, neither an EU membership nor a NATO membership should therefore be categorically excluded. At the same time, Ukraine deserves respect and support if it chooses to follow the wise path so successfully adopted by Finland.

We will have to be careful to address issues affecting the future European security architecture without conceding that we accept the annexation of Crimea, or the so-called "Putin doctrine." Of course, that is going to be difficult. But defending our positions while at the same time advocating engagement is not, and must not be, mutually exclusive. Instead, both go together: that is what a double strategy is all about.

Conclusion

If EU foreign policy has been dominated by concerns about the financial, economic, and political future of the EU, 2014 has clearly brought foreign and defense policy back to the top of the agenda. The current crisis can serve as a catalyst for Europe, both politically and militarily. With the new team in place in Brussels, the EU should start working on a new European Security Strategy. The last one, agreed to in 2003 (!), stems from a time when the world was quite different. This is not only true for the new challenge posed by a revisionist Russia, but also for other radical changes in the European neighborhood, including the impact of the energy revolution, the security risks in the Middle East, and the increased role of rising powers.

However, while we need a stronger Europe, the current crisis also demonstrates how important it is for the United States to remain a European power. A strong U.S. engagement and a clear commitment by all members to NATO is a *conditio sine qua non* for deterring a revisionist Russia from shaking up additional parts of Europe, from Moldova to Georgia. On a more positive note, the current crisis has underscored what still unites the transatlantic partners. Despite serious difficulties in transatlantic relations, especially between Berlin and Washington after the numerous revelations in the spying affair, which has dealt a severe blow to German trust in U.S. leadership, this is something we need to preserve and nurture for the future. Looking at the rather mute response from new powers such as China, India, and Brazil to the Ukraine crisis, we need to understand that the stability of the liberal international order built after 1945 must not be taken for granted. It needs continuous commitment from the United States, Canada, and their European partners. And it is also in this respect that Prime Minister Yatsenyuk makes a key point: the West staying united is what matters most—both for the future of Ukraine and for the future of the liberal world order.

Wolfgang Ischinger has been Chairman of the Munich Security Conference (MSC) and Global Head of Public Policy and Economic Research, Allianz SE/Munich, since 2008. He is an adjunct professor at the University of Tuebingen, and serves on the boards of numerous non-profit-institutions, including SIPRI/Stockholm, SWP/Berlin, AICGS/Washington, DC, and the American Academy, Berlin. A German career diplomat, he was State Secretary (Deputy Foreign Minister) from 1998 to 2001. From 2001 to 2006, he was the Federal Republic of Germany's Ambassador to the U.S., and from 2006 to 2008, to the Court of St James'. He represented the European Union in the Troika negotiations on the future of Kosovo in 2007, and in 2014, representing the OSCE Chairman-in-Office, he co-moderated Round Table discussions in Ukraine in order to promote a broad national dialogue.

Part 3

CHAPTER 4

Sino-Russian Relations

Kevin Rudd
Senior Fellow, Belfer Center for Science and
International Affairs
John F. Kennedy School of Government
Harvard University

CHAPTER 5

The Unconventional Energy Boom:
Bad Timing for a Revanchist Russia

Meghan L. O'Sullivan
Jeane Kirkpatrick Professor of the Practice of
International Affairs
John F. Kennedy School of Government
Harvard University

"As Xi is likely to remain the Chinese president at least until 2023 and Putin conceivably until 2024, the quality of the personal relationship between these two leaders is of crucial importance to the strategic relationship between the two countries. And thus far it is more than positive, as a reflection of both interests and temperament."

—KEVIN RUDD

Sino-Russian Relations

Kevin Rudd
Senior Fellow, Belfer Center for Science and International Affairs
John F. Kennedy School of Government
Harvard University

There are deep symbolic and substantive changes underway in Sino-Russian relations. These have not simply occurred since the appointment of Xi Jinping as the general secretary of the Chinese Communist Party and the return of Vladimir Putin as the Russian president. These changes have been underway for the better part of the decade, but they have now intensified.

- The key analytical question is what interests are driving this new, closer Sino-Russian relationship, and are there overriding limitations to these interests that will constrain the further elaboration of a form of strategic condominium between Beijing and Moscow?

- A further question is what impact does it likely have on the exercise of U.S. power globally, regionally, and institutionally?

National interests

The Chinese leadership does few things by accident. The fact that Russia was the first destination for Xi's first visit abroad as Chinese president in March 2013, barely a few weeks after assuming the office of president, was designed to make a point, both to China's domestic audience as well as to Russia and the wider international community. During that visit, Xi told his Russian counterpart that Beijing and Moscow should "resolutely support each other in efforts to protect national sovereignty, security, and development interests." Xi also promised to "closely coordinate in international regional affairs." And Putin reciprocated by saying that "the strategic partnership between us is of great importance on both a bilateral and global scale."[1]

Chinese interests

Arguably the strongest Chinese national interest with Russia had already been secured a quarter of a century ago when Deng and Gorbachev effectively resolved the outstanding border dispute, which had plagued the relationship between the two countries for centuries. Given China's deep, historical sensitivity to the stability of its border regions, and given that China shares borders with 14 other states (more than any other country in the world other than Russia itself, which also has 14), the fact that China's common border with Russia is now resolved, while many of its other land borders are not, is of profound significance to strategic perceptions in Beijing. This sense of strategic comfort is reinforced by the fact that China now has maritime border disputes with all its maritime neighbors in the East and South China Seas, including, of course, the unique circumstances pertaining to Taiwan. Furthermore, the fact that China has to worry much less about the integrity of the second longest of all its borders, both land and maritime (only the Mongolian border is longer), means that China is free to concentrate its diplomatic and military efforts elsewhere across its periphery and beyond. It has also created over the last couple of decades sufficient positive political, economic, and diplomatic space to construct a new relationship between these two historical rivals.

China also views Russia as an important strategic and diplomatic partner in prosecuting its global agenda to develop a multi-polar global order in the future. This is most apparent through the high level of political cooperation and coordination we see between Russia and China in the UN Security Council, the BRICS, the G20, and other global fora, although, as discussed below, there are also limits to this cooperation. China's commitment to a multi-polar order is not simply rhetorical. It has been part of the framework of Chinese foreign policy from the beginning of the PRC. At a more concrete level, China's commitment to multi-polarity is also a means by which it seeks counter-balance and, where necessary, checks American power across the councils of the world.

China's economic interests in Russia at this stage are almost unidimensional—how to secure China's long-term energy security without becoming even more dependent on the strategic choke points of the Strait of Hormuz and the Strait of Malacca. Energy security is one of the core, continuing agenda items for the Standing Committee of the Political Bureau. Within this context, the hard bargain China drove with Vladimir Putin during the latter's recent visit to China on long-term gas supply, resulting in an apparently highly discounted price, reflects deep and continuing Chinese national interests in energy security, even if this meant applying price pressure on the Russians at their most politically vulnerable point in the negotiating process.

China's military interests have also been served by securing access to Russian defense technologies and weapon systems. Again, this part of the relationship is not without its irritations given Russian accusations about Chinese breaches of intellectual property. Nonetheless, the trade has expanded and has provided China with access to capabilities that would have taken much longer to develop domestically.

The Chinese Navy (PLAN) also sees strategic value in participating in joint drills with Russian naval units. China and Russia held their biggest joint naval exercise ever in the Sea of Japan last year ("Joint Sea 2013"), to which China reportedly sent four destroyers, two guided missile frigates, and a support ship, while Russia dispatched 11 surface ships, including a guided-missile cruiser, and a submarine. The two navies also held "Joint Sea 2014" this year in the maritime and air zones in the East China Sea. According to the Chinese Defense Ministry: "China-Russia military cooperation shows high-level mutual trust," and the comprehensive strategic and cooperative partnership between China and Russia has entered a new period. Finally, China benefits indirectly from an activist Russian foreign policy in Central Europe, the Middle East, and elsewhere where Russia is acting against U.S. interests, for the simple reason that Russia keeps the U.S. strategically preoccupied in theaters beyond East Asia.[2]

Russian interests

Russian officials will gladly tell visiting foreigners that the current state of Russia-China relations is the best in the past 450 years. There are often, however, more guarded comments by Russian officials in private conversations, with some questioning how long all this will last, and what will happen when China begins more openly to call the shots in the relationship, rather than the reverse.

Russia shares with China a deep sense of strategic relief that their common border is no longer the subject of diplomatic acrimony or military confrontation. This enables Moscow to look less defensively to the east, where it can instead focus on fostering economic development across the vast Russian Far East, given its small population, large land mass, and as yet underdeveloped regional economy. A secure eastern border also enables Russia to focus its diplomacy and military effort along other frontiers of more immediate strategic concern, such as Ukraine, Georgia, and

Eastern Europe, as well as on its own domestic Islamic insurgency in Chechnya. Russia also shares with China a common and deepening concern about militant Islamism in southeastern Russia and western China, most particularly Xinjiang.

Russia and China have a deep strategic interest in the development of a more multi-polar global order. Russia sees China not just as a useful, but now as a critical partner in the UN Security Council in securing Russian interests in multiple theaters around the world, from Syria to Ukraine. Russia also perceives China as having now obtained the credibility with the G77 that Russia once had, providing, therefore, an ability to leverage some of this support to pursue its own interests across the broader multilateral agenda. For Russia, its emerging strategic partnership with China also directly provides Moscow with a diplomatic force multiplier against the United States and a broader diplomatic front from which to curb unilateral U.S. behavior.

Economically, the Chinese market represents an opportunity to rebirth the Russian economy. The growing complementarity between Russia's vast energy resources on the one hand and China's vast energy demand on the other represents what both sides would describe as a "win-win relationship." Russia has thus far not been a significant beneficiary of Chinese foreign direct investment, but there are strong signs indicating this will soon begin to change. By contrast, bilateral trade has exploded in the last decade from negligible numbers to nearly 100 billion USD. For China, this is useful. For Russia, it is critical.

Russia also sees China as providing an escape valve from the increasing threat and reality of Western financial sanctions, including Europe. Given the likely trajectory of Russia's relationships with the U.S. and the EU in the period ahead due to the deepening crisis in Ukraine, Russia will attach greater and greater priority to China and Chinese financial institutions' ability to "fill the gap" over time. Although it remains an open question whether China has the political will or financial capacity to fulfill this role to the extent Russia may desire.

Political personalities

Beyond the concrete nature of these intersecting national interests also lies the key question of the personalities of and personal relationships between the Russian and Chinese presidents. Both see themselves as strong, nationalist leaders. Both see themselves as defending their respective national values, which they publicly hold to be in contrast with those of the U.S. and the West. Both have a deep ideological and equally pragmatic commitment to the principle of mutual noninterference, which again they hold in contrast to U.S. and Western claims to assert universalist value propositions that apply to all states. While President Putin is of the Russian intelligence service, President Xi is deeply of the tradition of the PLA, his father having served as a revolutionary commander before liberation as well as his own brief PLA service as private secretary to China's then Defense Minister Geng Biao. As Xi is likely to remain the Chinese president at least until 2023 and Putin conceivably until 2024, the quality of the personal relationship between these two leaders is of crucial importance to the strategic relationship between the two countries. And thus far it is more than positive, as a reflection of both interests and temperament.

Limitations to Sino-Russian condominium

There are, nonetheless, many limitations to the future scope of Sino-Russian relations that must be equally recognized. First, there are long national historiographies within each country about the other that are almost universally and deeply negative. In the long history of the relationship, it's important to remember that: "one swallow doth not a summer make."

Second, for Russia, despite the resolution of the border, there is still a deep sense of strategic anxiety about its unpopulated Russian Far East. Russian politicians are also susceptible to sensationalist media reporting in Russia about "Chinese hordes" pouring across an unguarded border under the camouflage of trade and commerce, although the reality is that border crossings are relatively small in number and well regulated. But this does not diminish the salience of the issue in Russian domestic politics. The Russian Duma can be particularly sensitive on such matters.

Third, there is also deep and unresolved concern in both Beijing and Moscow about future strategic competition in Central Asia. The dimensions of this are relatively clear. Kazakhstan in particular finds itself to be the meat in the sandwich. Whereas Kazakhstan has become an inaugural member of the Eurasian Union with Russia, there is also a deep recognition in Astana (and Moscow) of the long-term magnetic force represented by the overwhelming presence of the Chinese economy. Each of these tensions is being played out in a different way in the other four Central Asian republics. Given the relevance of Central Asia to Russia's geopolitical interests on the one hand and China's long-term economic and energy interests on the other, there is likely to be continuing competition, albeit undeclared, for strategic influence, energy access, and transportation corridors across all five Central Asian republics.

Fourth, multilaterally, as indicated above, there are also likely to be limitations on the extent to which China will automatically support all future Russian initiatives or requirements in the UN Security Council. There are concerns within China about the extent to which China's global reputation over time may become increasingly negatively impacted by automatically supporting Russia in the Council. Such support becomes particularly difficult on issues such as Ukraine, given that China has a substantive relationship with Kiev. Furthermore, China will always be predisposed toward a conservative position on territorial integrity and political sovereignty of an individual state, including on issues such as Ukraine. China will always be mindful of any precedents being set that would potentially impact its own long-term national interests in relation to external interference in Taiwan, Xinjiang, and Tibet. For these reasons, China chose to abstain in the vote of the UN Security Council resolution on Ukraine in March 2014.

Finally, China, given its own domestic air pollution crisis as well as its direct experience of the early impacts of climate change, is likely to become more globally active in climate change negotiations than Russia. In fact, China may be more likely to find core strategic common purpose with the United States in taking significant national (and therefore global) action on greenhouse gas emissions. China will need, for its own national interests, to see global carbon emissions come down for fear that they will fundamentally disrupt China's economic rise in the decades ahead. Therefore, combined action by China and the U.S., as the world's two largest polluters, will become increasingly critical for Chinese interests in the future. Russia, by contrast, given its historical dependence on carbon exports, has not been a proactive player in the global climate change negotiations. Furthermore, China's determination to radically reduce the carbon intensity of its total energy mix in the future may also have a long-term impact on China's global demand for nonrenewable energy, including from Russia.

Conclusion

The key element in the emerging Sino-Russian relationship is what Beijing and Moscow respectively seek, and believe they can secure, in their future relationship with the world's remaining super power, the United States.

This has long been a triangular strategic relationship. Sino-Soviet strategic cooperation against the U.S. barely lasted for a decade after the founding of the

People's Republic. There then followed a decade of what might be called strategic equidistance between Moscow, Beijing, and Washington, during which China turned inward and went through the ravages of the Cultural Revolution. This in turn was followed by Nixon's rapprochement with China, which cemented strategic cooperation between China and the United States against the Soviet Union until the Soviet collapse 20 years later.

In many respects, this "anti-Sovietism" constituted the core strategic rationale for Sino-U.S. relations throughout this period, masking the absence of any other significant, positive strategic rationale that could supersede it. Therefore, when the reason for this strategic cooperation collapsed along with the collapse of the Soviet Union itself, it was not replaced by a succeeding strategic rationale to provide a new long-term basis for the U.S.-China relationship. Arguably, the U.S.-China relationship has been increasingly strategically adrift for the last 20 years in the absence of a new compelling rationale, other than mutual economic advantage. Meanwhile, over the last decade, the U.S.-Russian relationship has steadily deteriorated—particularly since the U.S. invasion of Iraq and the continuing debate concerning NATO expansion to include Ukraine and Georgia. This period has in turn seen Russia embarking on a new strategic and foreign policy direction itself. At the same time, the broad strategic circumstances were gradually being created for the beginning of a Sino-Russian rapprochement, made possible by the resolution of the border dispute during the previous decade.

Nonetheless, the strategic and operational question remains: Will the emerging elements of a Sino-Russia strategic cooperation and/or condominium increasingly impair U.S. freedom for independent military and diplomatic maneuver on the global and regional stage? Certainly, the limitations to Chinese and Russian strategic cooperation are real. Nonetheless, it would be a grave misreading by the United States if it concluded that China and Russia are somehow fundamentally incapable of deepening and broadening their regional and global strategic cooperation in the future, given the interests they share, the absence of natural allies elsewhere, and the chemistry that currently prevails in the personal relationship between the two leaders.

The central organizing principle of Sino-Russian strategic cooperation, both for the past decade and most probably for the next, lies in their common strategic distrust of the United States. In other words, "my enemy's enemy is my friend." And whereas the Sino-Russian relationship will over time become increasingly one-sided (with the single, continuing, and significant exception being the size of their respective strategic nuclear arsenals, where Russia will remain dominant), their combined capacity to complicate, frustrate, impede, and thwart the unilateral deployment of American power will become increasingly significant.

Kevin Rudd served as Australia's 26th Prime Minister from 2007 to 2010, then as Foreign Minister from 2010 to 2012, before returning to the Prime Ministership in 2013. As Prime Minister, he led Australia's response during the Global Financial Crisis. He is also internationally recognized as one of the founders of the G20. Prime Minister Rudd remains engaged in a range of international challenges including global economic management, the rise of China, climate change, and sustainable development. In February 2014, he was named a Senior Fellow with Harvard University's John F. Kennedy School of Government. Harvard has asked him to undertake a major research project on Alternative Futures for U.S.-China Relations for the Next Decade. Prime Minister Rudd is on the International Advisory Panel of Chatham House. He is a proficient speaker of Mandarin Chinese, a Visiting Professor at Tsinghua University and funded the establishment of the Australian Centre on China in the World at the Australian National University. He was a co-author of the report of the UN Secretary General's High Level Panel on Global Sustainability–"Resilient People, Resilient Planet" and chairs the World Economic Forum's Global Agenda Council on Fragile States. He also remains actively engaged in indigenous reconciliation.

[1] Gelb, Leslie H., Dimitri K. Sime. July-August 2013. "Beware Collusion of China, Russia." *The National Interest*. http://nationalinterest.org/article/beware-collusion-china-russia-8640.

[2] Guo, Renjie, ed. May 29, 2014. "DM Spokesman: China-Russia Military Cooperation Shows High-Level Mutual Trust." *China Military Online*. http://eng.mod.gov.cn/Press/2014-05/29/content_4512828.htm.

"Almost certainly, Putin will need to look for other ways to legitimize his rule as the substantial improvement in living standards that Russians have experienced during his leadership stalls and potentially reverses; adventurism abroad will have the dual benefit of increasing Putin's credibility in Russian eyes and adding geopolitical risk to the global price of oil. "

—MEGHAN L. O'SULLIVAN

The Unconventional Energy Boom:
Bad Timing for a Revanchist Russia

Meghan L. O'Sullivan[1]
Jeane Kirkpatrick Professor of the Practice of
International Affairs
John F. Kennedy School of Government
Harvard University

Yegor Gaidar, a leading Russian policymaker and economist at the time of the dissolution of the Soviet Union, offered an alternative to the common American narrative about what led to the empire's demise. Rather than giving President Reagan or the United States credit, Gaidar attributes the collapse—as well as the peaceful manner in which Moscow let events in Eastern Europe unfold—to persistently low oil prices. If Gaidar were alive today, would he be predicting gloom and doom for Russia in the face of the dramatic changes occurring in the energy realm currently underway?

The revolution in unconventional energy has altered the global energy landscape. New technologies in the extraction of oil and gas have transformed the U.S. energy profile, making America now nearly self-sufficient in natural gas and offering the medium-term prospect of energy self-sufficiency. Although commercial production of unconventional oil and gas is currently limited to the United States and Canada, several other countries have the potential to make equally significant contributions to global supplies over the years ahead.

Given Russia's dependence on energy for its domestic development and the role of energy in its foreign policy, today's new energy dynamics will influence both Russia's strategies and its prospects at home and abroad. It is critical for Russian policymakers—and U.S. ones looking to anticipate Russian behavior in the months and years ahead—to understand how the unconventional revolution will affect Russia, how Russia will react to the new pressures created, and how this cocktail of events will affect Russia's geopolitical orientation. While there are many unknowns that will impact the specific course of future events, one can already discern the broad contours of the unconventional energy boom and its impact on Russia. On the whole, this revolution will create added hardships for Russia and diminish its traditional use of energy as a political tool. But rather than pushing Russia into a more accommodating state, such difficulties could reinforce Russian petulance.

The effects of the unconventional energy revolution on Russia

As a graduate student, Vladimir Putin submitted a dissertation titled "The Strategic Planning of Regional Resources Under the Formation of Market Relations" in which he emphasized the importance of resource power and linked it directly to national power.[2] Claims of plagiarism aside, the thesis foreshadowed what would eventually become defining elements of Putin's domestic and foreign policy initiatives.

While most observers appreciate the importance of fossil fuels to Russia's economy, few may be aware of how it has increased significantly under Putin's rule. By 2013, 68 percent of Russia's export revenue came from the sale of crude oil, petroleum products, and natural gas (33 percent, 21 percent, and 14 percent, respectively).[3] The total value of these exports was $350 billion and represented almost 50 percent of total federal budget revenues in 2013.[4] Even more telling, revenues from oil and gas products had constituted only 15.4 percent of the Russian budget 10 years prior and less than 2 percent two decades prior.

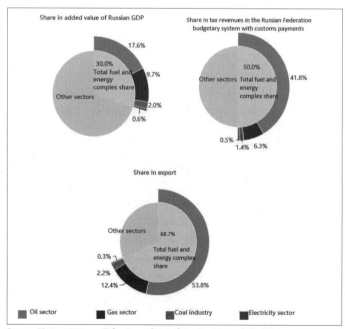

Source: Tatiana Mitrova, "The Geopolitics of Russian Natural Gas," February 2014

The unconventional boom is influencing Russia's energy sector and economy in significant ways. Although not an exhaustive list, the impact of the unconventional revolution on Russia can be attributed to three factors: its effect on the oil price and Russia's growth model; its actual and potential impact on Russia's markets, particularly in Europe; and the threats it has created to the long-standing convention of indexing natural gas prices to the price of oil.

Although few Russians will make the connection, the unconventional boom occurring in the United States and Canada bears significant responsibility for ending the energy-driven growth model that Russia has followed for more than a decade. Since 2003, Russia has experienced an almost continuous rise in GDP and GDP per capita; this growth has been fueled by the near-steady rise in global oil prices.

Consistently rising oil prices also spared Russia and its leaders the hard work of diversifying their economy away from its reliance on fossil fuels. With the exception of a brief period in 2008 and 2009, when the global oil price temporarily plunged to $41, rising oil prices from 2001-2011 virtually exempted the Russian leadership from undertaking broad energy and economic reforms.[5]

This "effortless" growth slowed dramatically with the stabilization of the price of oil over the last three years, which can in large part be traced to the unconventional revolution.[6] In the last five years, U.S. production of "tight" oil has swelled, adding approximately 3 million barrels per day to global supply.[7] This supply, coincidentally, more than equals the amount of oil that came off the global market in the same time period due to politically induced production disruptions in Iran, Sudan, Libya, and Syria.[8]

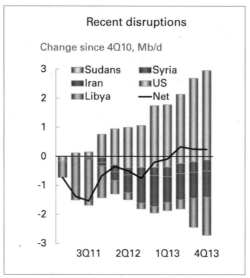

Source: BP Energy Outlook 2035

Although it is impossible to predict exactly what the price of oil would have been in the absence of the U.S. unconventional production, one can say with certainty that it would have been higher than it was, likely allowing Russia to continue its energy-driven growth at least for a while longer. Analysis by Trevor Houser and Shashank Mohan suggests that in the absence of the North American unconventional boom, the global price of oil would be 3-11 percent higher throughout 2013 to 2035.[9] For Russia, this "loss" in the oil price translates to somewhere between $7.9 to 28.9 billion a year at 2012 production and export levels, all other things equal.

The impact of the unconventional revolution on global energy prices—and therefore, the Russian economy—may only be in its early phases. It is conceivable that global oil supply—spurred by U.S. tight oil production and/or production from other countries seeking to exploit their unconventional resources—will outstrip lower than expected global demand or impede OPEC's ability to keep oil prices close to current levels. If so, global oil prices could fall, perhaps not to as low as they did in the 1980s or even 2008, but to $70 or $80, which is the price at which some unconventional production would be suspended. The price Russia receives for its gas, although not set on a global market like that of oil, also has been and will continue to be influenced by the unconventional boom as discussed below.

In addition to affecting price and arresting the Russian growth model of the past decade, the unconventional boom poses a challenge to Russia's ability to maintain its markets for energy exports. The fact that Russia is now concerned about markets for its gas is a dramatic shift from the much friendlier landscape that Russia inhabited only 10 years ago when its primary concern was to produce sufficient gas to meet its internal needs and external commitments.[10]

Russia's current preoccupation about maintaining its gas markets abroad has many roots, including stagnating European demand, but the shale gale is an important factor. Already, the impact is tangible, if not acute. Looking back to 2007, Russia had grand plans to develop Shtokman, a massive natural gas field in the South Barents Sea containing an estimated 3.9 trillion cubic meters of gas reserves.[11] This complex, expensive project was intended to meet the needs of what was anticipated by all to be the growing natural gas import needs of the United States. The emergence of shale gas on the American scene made the United States nearly self-sufficient in natural gas, eliminating the need for $20 billion dollar projects like Shtokman, which was cancelled in 2012 (with write-offs totaling over $300 million for Statoil alone).[12]

The shale gale in the United States has posed other, less direct—but potentially more nerve-wracking—challenges to Russia's main market: Europe. In 2012, 79 percent of Russia's crude oil exports were shipped to Europe, with Germany, the Netherlands, and Poland the largest individual customers.[13] In the same year, Russia was exporting almost 50 percent of its gas products to EU customers.[14] West African liquefied natural gas (LNG) once destined for U.S. markets sought other destinations, finding a home in Europe in 2009 and 2010 until higher Asian prices pulled it eastward. And American coal—which some Russian analysts refer to as "indirect LNG"—displaced by more economical U.S. natural gas made its way to European markets, substituting for higher priced natural gas.[15]

Thus far, these challenges to Russia's gas market in Europe remain marginal. However, they have the potential to rise significantly, in conjunction with other factors and depending on choices that European and even American policymakers make in the months and years ahead. Many on both sides of the Atlantic have heralded the potential for Europe to displace Russian gas with imports of American LNG. There are, however, significant obstacles to this occurring. Most importantly, the price differential between the U.S. and European markets is unlikely sufficient to motivate *large* quantities of natural gas to flow to Europe; after all, neither American nor European companies that sell and buy the gas will be motivated by non-commercial considerations when striking a deal. The market will move most of the U.S. LNG expected to come on line to Asian markets, where the price is significantly higher than in Europe and the United States. Europe could decide that it is willing to pay a premium for the security of U.S. gas; if it were willing to subsidize the purchase of U.S. LNG in some fashion, then American exports could make greater inroads. While not an impossible scenario to imagine, Europe has not yet shown that it is willing to pay higher prices for the same commodity; the lowest price gas (Russian piped gas) has generally won out over potential competitors.

Finally, the shale revolution is challenging the practice of indexing gas prices to oil prices, another long-standing cornerstone of Russia's energy strategy. While it makes little sense today, this approach began in the 1960s when oil and oil products were more substitutes for gas than they are today. European and Asian consumers have grown less fond of this arrangement as oil prices have seemed to hew to new fundamentals (with China's voracious appetite for energy); they have become more envious of their U.S. counterparts as natural gas prices in America—which are set, in contrast, by gas-on-gas competition—plunged as shale gas came on line. The flow of new LNG once destined for U.S. markets into Europe in 2009 and 2010 gave European utilities leverage to renegotiate their contracts with Gazprom. In some instances, the utilities were able to compel the Russian behemoth to incorporate spot prices into the formula for determining the price at which it sells gas and to ease "take or pay" clauses. Such pressures for renegotiation continue and are likely to intensify once the United States begins exporting its natural gas in 2015 or 2016; as the three existing natural gas markets of North America, Asia, and Europe become more interconnected due to the increased flow of LNG, European customers will have even more leverage in their negotiations with Gazprom. Such dynamics and trends suggest that, even if Russia maintains its European gas market, it will earn less from the same volumes of sales.

Russian reaction to the unconventional revolution

Russia, and Gazprom in particular, was slow to appreciate the significance of the shale boom and to assess its consequences for Russia. For years, Russian policymakers and industry analysts dismissed the phenomenon as "a fad" or a "bubble about to burst." The first real public acknowledgement of the challenges that the shale gale posed to Russia was made in August 2012, when Russian Energy Minister Novak addressed reporters and declared the need to adjust Russia's energy strategy in light of the new technologies to extract shale.[16] Nevertheless, today, many Russians still question the sustainability of the boom and its ability to affect prices or other fundamentals.

There is, however, some evidence that Russia has incorporated new elements in its approach as a result of the unconventional boom. Although Gazprom has followed a policy aimed at maximizing gas prices over keeping market share, as mentioned above, it has reluctantly yielded on its insistence of oil-indexation, renegotiating the pricing formula in some European contracts and, at least for the moment, accepting a lower price for its gas.[17]

Russia has also embarked on its own efforts to develop its supposedly vast quantities of unconventional oil; the EIA estimates that Russia has 75 billion barrels of shale oil reserves, the largest in the world. Russia has put in place tax breaks and other incentives to develop such basins, and Rosneft recently signed agreements with BP and Exxon to join it in this effort. While such efforts are a sensible investment in Russia's resource future, given the nature of the resource, few expect that Russia will be producing huge quantities of unconventional oil at competitive prices in the short or medium run.

Perhaps even more interesting is how the unconventional energy revolution and the more recent crisis with the West over Ukraine have combined to add serious urgency to earlier elements of Russia's energy strategy. First, these two factors dramatically increased the intensity with which Russia is pursuing the development of its resources in Eastern Siberia and the capture of Asia's growing markets. The Russian government has long aspired to develop Siberia to add economic viability and population density to vast expanses of barely populated land so close to the crowded Chinese border area. Moreover, as Russia's legacy oil fields in Western Siberia have declined, the need to develop greenfield projects out east has become even more pressing.

The unconventional revolution, however, catapulted these goals to develop Russia's east from being desirable to urgent. Suddenly, the burgeoning gas markets of Asia looked as if they would have multiple supply options to meet their gas needs in the not too distant future. On account of the shale gale, significant U.S. and Canadian LNG shipments to Asia are expected in the next couple of years, and huge Australian projects are also poised to tip more LNG into the market. While gas demand in Asia will be robust under any scenario, China's own enormous shale gas reserves and its efforts to develop them also raise question marks around the demand equation. Russia clearly needed to lock in Asian demand for its resources as soon as possible.

Complementing this realization was the crisis over Ukraine, which provided definitive proof that Europe would never welcome the closer integration of Europe and Russia that many Russian analysts insist Putin originally sought. The role that energy played in this latest confrontation all but ensured a more robust effort from

Europe to diminish the leverage that Russia wielded over it in time. Long-standing U.S. efforts to help Europe meet its gas needs independent of Russia would certainly intensify. The geopolitical realities supplemented the economic rationales for "going east." It is no coincidence that after more than a decade of negotiation about the details—just months after the annexation of Crimea—Russia and China signed a deal to send 38 billion cubic meters of Russian gas to China each year through pipelines and from fields that need to be built and developed from scratch.

The combined impetuses from the Ukraine crisis and the unconventional revolution also lent greater urgency to the long-held plan to finalize and complete the South Stream pipeline from Anapa, Russia, to Varna, Bulgaria, and potentially extending it as far as Austria or Northern Italy.[18] In addition to circumventing Ukraine, Russia sees the completion of South Stream as a way of guaranteeing European demand for its gas over the long run and making the development of more expensive European shale gas even less attractive. If Gazprom builds all four pipeline legs to the project, the South Stream could supply an additional 63 billion cubic meters of natural gas to Europe, completely eliminating the need to transit gas for the continent through Ukraine.

The biggest outstanding question about Russia's reaction to the unconventional boom is whether these externally driven changes in global energy markets will be a driver of Russian reform. Before the Ukraine crisis transformed prospects for relations between Russia and the West, one might have predicted that the cumulative effect of the energy revolution would be to spur greater reform in Russia. In more competitive global markets, Gazprom would need to be leaner and more efficient, something perhaps only conceivable if greater competition were introduced within Russia's internal gas market. In fact, several developments in recent years suggested a movement in this direction. For instance, "independent" companies such as Novatek and Rosneft became significant players in the internal market, competing with Gazprom for domestic consumers. Over the past decade, the Russian government began a gradual liberalization of domestic gas prices, an effort that was suspended in 2013. In the final months of 2013, Putin himself instituted a significant change to the long-standing policy that has given Gazprom a monopoly over the sale of all energy abroad; Novatek was given permission to export LNG from its Yamal project to Asia. In a lower price environment (one result of the unconventional boom), Russia production (and resultant government revenues) might depend increasingly on efficiency, less corruption, and technology that comes from abroad; reforming the system to be more transparent, less arbitrary, and more welcoming of foreign investment would be essential.

This logic in favor of reform, however, must be tempered by political reality. In the absence of Russia's crisis with the West, reform might be a predictable outcome of the unconventional boom. But events of the past months make dramatic reform highly unlikely, even if economic pressures would suggest otherwise. One expert, close to the Russian government, said that Gazprom would only be reformed "when it is a risk-free proposition," which could be another way of saying that Gazprom will never reform.[19] Such reforms carry particular risk at a time when Russia is on questionable economic and international footing. They could undermine Putin's mechanisms for delivering patronage to his networks and could eliminate the need for Putin as an arbitrator of a corrupt and capricious system. Moreover, in the current international climate, such reforms could conceivably bring no benefits from external actors, who may not be able to respond to a more positive investment climate due to sanctions or other punitive policies. Remembering the unanticipated events and eventual collapse first set in motion by Gorbachev, Putin is unlikely to opt for dramatic reforms in today's political environment, even if the unconventional revolution suggests the need for them.

Geopolitical implications

Although many factors will affect Russia's behavior in the months and years ahead, the global energy system will be a significant determinant given the central role of energy in Russia. The unconventional energy boom has prompted and will continue to spur a number of geopolitical shifts, many of them related to Russia. The shale boom is driving Russia to overcome long-standing tensions with China, possibly opening the door for a more strategic partnership between the two countries, which could pose challenges to the United States. It is affecting Russia's interaction with the Central Asian republics, which are seen now more as competitors than essential suppliers to Russia. And the unconventional boom has affected the viability of the Gas Exporting Countries Forum (GEFC)—a plan to create an OPEC-like cartel among gas producers.

From the perspective of many countries, however, the two most consequential geopolitical implications of the unconventional boom are its ability to affect Russian domestic stability and the extent to which it influences Russia's ability to use energy as a weapon vis-à-vis Europe. As discussed above, the unconventional boom creates economic hardship for Russia. At a minimum, it has disrupted its economic growth model; the Russian government and international institutions—even before the crisis over Ukraine—had downgraded expectations for growth over the next one to five years, with recessionary effects expected to be seen by the end of 2014.[20] Russia has already needed to renegotiate downward the price it receives for some of its gas, although the potential for more significant adjustments lies in the future. At a maximum, downward pressures on oil prices—by no means certain but well in the realm of the feasible— could be catastrophic.[21] Today, Russia needs to fetch approximately $117 a barrel for its oil to cover its budget expenditures[22]—a number that already reflects some cuts in the budget by the government.[23]

How would Russia weather significantly lower revenues? In the Soviet days, Moscow turned to hard currency, gold reserves, foreign borrowing, and increased printing of money to finance increasingly large deficits.[24] Today, Russia is able to utilize its sovereign wealth stabilization fund (consisting of a reserve fund and a national well-being fund) to help it withstand any temporary drop in prices or to otherwise finance budget deficits that the country may encounter.[25] However, estimates by the Russian Academy of Sciences suggest that more than a year of oil prices at $70 per barrel would be enough to exhaust Russia's financial reserves; even more modest drops in oil prices could lead to substantial capital flight out of Russia.[26] Should prices drop to $75, where they would force out some (but not all) of the unconventional production, for a prolonged period, the economic situation could begin to impinge on domestic political stability in a variety of ways.

Extreme political scenarios are plausible, although still unlikely barring a prolonged dip in prices and the confluence of some additional events. Putin could struggle to maintain the political system he has constructed, which is based on the satisfaction of elites and his inner circle, leading to political fragmentation and a threat to the viability of his regime. In the absence of an alternative patron, however, Putin's inner circle would be reluctant to abandon Putin, as their fates are closely tied to his destiny; it is not only carrots that make this system work, but the stick of what would occur to this group should the current system deteriorate. Alternatively, a much more difficult economic situation could be destabilizing at a popular level, leading to protests beyond the scale of those that have occurred in the past—inviting either a collapse of Putin's rule similar to what occurred in Ukraine or a resort to unprecedented repression by the regime.

Less dramatic, but still worrying, scenarios are more feasible. Moscow could lose some of its ability to influence events in the regions, resulting in security problems emanating from places such as the Northern Caucuses, where 60 percent to 80 percent of the regional budgets are comprised of subsidies from the federal government.[27] Almost certainly, Putin will need to look for other ways to legitimize his rule as the substantial improvement in living standards that Russians have experienced during his leadership stalls and potentially reverses;[28] adventurism abroad will have the dual benefit of increasing Putin's credibility in Russian eyes and adding geopolitical risk to the global price of oil. Russia may look for other, less direct, ways to boost the price of oil—whether through stoking sectarian conflict in Syria and Iraq or thwarting an international deal with Iran.

Looking to other facets of its external behavior, Russia will find it more difficult to use energy as a political tool in its relations with Europe—and Europe will be less constrained by its energy needs in confronting Russia. This changed reality, however, will not be because Europe is able to displace Russian gas with its own production of shale gas and imports of American LNG. Trends and volumes just do not suggest this is possible, even with a major European and American push in this direction.

Although Europe has considerable reserves of shale gas, its development has been slow and stymied in most cases by political barriers. In 2012, the International Energy Agency (IEA) in Paris estimated that even under the most favorable regulatory arrangements, the European Union's future production of unconventional gas would not fully compensate for the expected decline in European conventional production out to 2035.[29] To fully displace Russian gas, one analyst estimated that Europe would also need to dramatically increase its wind and solar capacity, significantly step up the efficiency of its buildings, embrace a nuclear renaissance, and maintain current levels of coal usage.[30] As mentioned earlier, some U.S. LNG will flow to Europe, but it is unlikely to do so in vast quantities as long as the high price of gas in Asia makes export to that region much more attractive than to Europe—or unless Europe decides that it is willing to pay a higher price for U.S. natural gas than for the Russian variety.

Reflecting these realities and challenges, most current projections suggest that Europe will remain dependent on Russian gas as its primary supplier. Worst case scenarios for unconventional production, renewable energy efforts, LNG imports, and a range of other factors all highlight the possibility that European dependency on Russian gas will actually rise in the coming years.[31]

The good news is that even if Russia maintains its dominant supplier position in Europe over the coming years, the unconventional revolution will give Europe more breathing room in managing this trade. First, as discussed above, the increasing interconnectedness of the three global gas markets and the growing spot market for gas will give Europe more leverage to move further away from the oil indexation and to negotiate better prices for its gas imports. Equally important, even if Europe does not choose to import LNG from the United States or elsewhere because it can acquire Russian gas for less, the emergence of the United States and Canada as significant LNG exporters creates real alternatives for Europe in a crisis situation. Today, some Europeans falsely look to the projected 77 billion cubic meters of excess capacity at European LNG terminals as a security blanket;[32] the current tightness of the global market for LNG, however, means that Europe would struggle to lure LNG from gas thirsty Asia today, even if it were willing to pay an extremely high price. In the coming years, U.S. LNG will add fluidity and liquidity to the market, making it conceivable that a distressed Europe could actually obtain LNG at a moment of crisis, if it were willing to pay higher prices.

If Europe is serious about maximizing the salutary effects of the unconventional boom for its security, it needs to think hard about how it ranks its three priorities of climate/environment, competitiveness, and energy security. Even the short discussion above demonstrates how energy security can be improved, but somewhat at the expense of one or both of the other priorities. For instance, Europe could seek alternative supplies of gas through new pipeline projects or by deciding to pay a security premium for the import of American LNG. These options will be more costly than continued reliance on Russian gas and therefore come at the expense of competitiveness. Encouraging more domestic shale production could at least help ensure that Russian market share in Europe does not increase in the future, but many governments would need to take a more permissive stance toward environmentally controversial practices. There are some lower hanging fruit, including increased efficiency of buildings, better interconnectors, reverse flow pipelines, and extra gas storage in Europe—all steps that are currently underway.

Finally, it is worth noting that Europe and the United States are not the only players whose actions determine what role energy will play in future EU-Russia relations. The actions of China, a massive actor in the energy realm, will reverberate globally and affect Europe's situation in many ways. For instance, should China agree to Russia's continued pressure to the proposed Altai pipeline, the implications for European energy security could be serious. In contrast to the gas pipeline just agreed to by Russia and China in May, the Altai pipeline would—for the first time—give Russia the opportunity to shift gas currently flowing to Europe to China. With this option, the "mutually assured destruction" that would come from the cessation of Russian gas exports to Europe today would no longer hold. In addition, China's efforts to develop its own shale—and Japan's decision about whether to return to nuclear power—will in many ways determine how lucrative the Asian market is for Russia and how viable an alternative it is to its traditional European market.

Conclusion

Overall, the unconventional revolution brings little for the Russians to celebrate—even in these early stages when shale production is largely limited to the United States and Canada. Through its dampening impact on oil and gas prices, it has contributed to the weakening of Russia's economy. It has complicated—although hardly eliminated—Russia's efforts to use energy as a political tool, either explicitly or implicitly. And it has forced Russia to prioritize and elevate elements of its energy strategy that are difficult, expensive, and have long time horizons. In conjunction with other political or economic developments, the unconventional revolution could even help pose a challenge to the viability of Putin's regime.

For Russia, there would be no good time for the unconventional revolution to take hold in the United States, much less abroad. But the dynamics unleashed by the shale gale are particularly problematic for a Russian leadership that seeks to re-exert itself on the global stage in a way reminiscent of Soviet days. The unconventional revolution creates added vulnerabilities for Russia at a time when the United States and others will be looking for them; for instance, the unconventional boom makes Russia's effort to capture eastern markets critical, but this drive east is also more dependent on foreign technology and, therefore, susceptible to sanctions and other pressures.

An optimist might predict that the unconventional revolution will curb problematic Russian behavior or lead Putin to be more pliable or less problematic. But rather than mitigating Putin's behavior, the added pressure could exacerbate it. The changed global energy dynamics will further strain internal problems, which may be compensated by external adventurism. In his handling of Ukraine, Putin has already demonstrated a willingness to bear economic pain in the interest of a wider political agenda; the crisis with Ukraine may also demonstrate Putin's willingness to distract the Russian population at home from economic distress by creating disturbances abroad. Finally, the unconventional revolution generates incentives for Putin to stir the pot internationally to maintain a high geopolitical premium in the price of oil. Unless new technologies or new political frameworks change the energy landscape in even more radical ways, the unconventional revolution will not be sufficient to cow Putin, but it may be adequate to further provoke him.

Meghan L. O'Sullivan is the Jeane Kirkpatrick Professor of the Practice of International Affairs and Director of the Geopolitics of Energy Project at Harvard University's Kennedy School of Government. In 2013, she served as the vice chair of the All Party Talks in Northern Ireland, which sought to resolve ongoing obstacles to peace. Between 2004 and 2007, she was special assistant to President George W. Bush and Deputy National Security Advisor for Iraq and Afghanistan during the last two years of her tenure. There, she helped run the 2006 strategic policy review on Iraq which led to the "surge" strategy. She spent two years in Iraq from 2003-2008. Dr. O'Sullivan is a columnist for Bloomberg View, an advisor to energy companies, and an adjunct senior fellow at the Council of Foreign Relations. She is a trustee of the German Marshall Fund and a member of the Trilateral Commission's Executive Committee and the Aspen Strategy Group and on an advisory committee at the George W. Bush Institute. She has been awarded the Defense Department's highest honor for civilians and, three times, the State Department's Superior Honor Award. She has a B.A. from Georgetown University and a master's and doctorate from Oxford University.

[1] I am grateful for the help and advice of Adam Papa and Morena Skalamera in preparing this article.

[2] Lynch, Allen. 2011. *Vladimir Putin and Russian Statecraft*. Sterling, VA: Potomac Books. p. 36-37.

[3] EIA. July 23, 2014. "Oil and Natural Gas Sales Accounted for 68% of Russia's Total Export Revenues in 2013." www.eia.gov/todayinenergy/detail.cfm?id=17231.

[4] Ibid.

[5] Data from: EIA. July 30, 2014. "Petroleum and Other Liquids: Spot Prices." www.eia.gov/dnav/pet/pet_pri_spt_s1_m.htm.

[6] Wilson, William T. May 19, 2014. "The Russian Economy Stares into the Abyss." Washington, DC: Heritage Foundation. www.heritage.org/research/reports/2014/05/the-russian-economy-stares-into-the-abyss. Data from EIA, www.eia.gov/dnav/pet/pet_pri_spt_s1_m.htm.

[7] EIA. May 30, 2014. "Overview Data for United States." www.eia.gov/countries/country-data.cfm?fips=us.

[8] BP. January 2014. *BP Energy Outlook to 2035*. www.bp.com/content/dam/bp/pdf/Energy-economics/Energy-Outlook/Energy_Outlook_2035_booklet.pdf.

[9] Houser, Trevor, and Shashank Mohan. 2014. *Fueling Up: The Economic Implications of America's Oil and Gas Boom*. Washington, DC: Peterson Institute for International Economics. p. 45.

[10] Data from: EIA. November 26, 2014. "Country Analysis Brief Overview: Russia." www.eia.gov/countries/country-data.cfm?fips=RS#ng.

[11] Belton, Catherine, and Guy Chazen. August 29, 2012. "Shtokman Exit Shows a Realistic Gazprom." *Financial Times*. www.ft.com/intl/cms/s/0/b6c8cf9c-f1f8-11e1-bba3-00144feabdc0.html?siteedition=uk#axzz3FCpzMd8z.

[12] Ibid; Gorst, Isabel. August 7, 2012. "Statoil: Wrong Partner, Wrong Place, Wrong Time," *Financial Times*. blogs.ft.com/beyond-brics/2012/08/07/statoil-wrong-partner-wrong-place-wrong-time/.

[13] EIA. March 12, 2014. "Russia: Overview." www.eia.gov/countries/cab.cfm?fips=rs.

[14] Observatory of Economic Complexity. "Learn More About Russian Trade." Cambridge, MA: MIT. atlas.media.mit.edu/profile/country/rus/.

[15] While American coal did make its way to Europe, the greater purchase of coal by Europe was probably even more a reflection of a slowdown in the rate of growth in the demand for coal in China.

[16] *Moscow Times*. August 31, 2012. "Ministry to Adjust Strategy Due to Shale Gas Boom." www.themoscowtimes.com/business/article/ministry-to-adjust-strategy-due-to-shale-gas-boom/467366.html.

[17] Russia points out, rightly, that incorporating spot pricing into the formula does not necessarily mean the price will always be lower. In the words of Alexander Medvedev, "We were faced with a choice: either to maintain volume and market share at whatever cost, or concentrate on maintaining revenue. As a public, profit-making enterprise, Gazprom OJSC is interested in increasing earnings, so as to ensure a profit for our shareholders. So the right choice was made—in favor of revenue, and the results support this. What's more, the system of long-term contracts with 'take-or-pay' conditions and the principle of pricing indexed to a basket of petroleum products, etc., were kept intact." Quoted in: Tatiana Mitrova. February 2014. "The Geopolitics of Russian Natural Gas." Harvard University's Belfer Center and Rice University's Baker Institute Center for Energy Studies. p. 64. http://belfercenter.hks.harvard.edu/files/CES-pub-GeoGasRussia-022114.pdf.

[18] "Gazprom and European gas markets: Paying the Piper." January 4, 2014. *The Economist*. www.economist.com/news/business/21592639-european-efforts-reduce-russian-state-owned-companys-sway-over-gas-prices-have-been.

[19] Interview by author, Moscow, May 28, 2014.

[20] Thompson, Mark. March 26, 2014. "Recession Warning for Russia." CNN. money.cnn.com/2014/03/26/news/economy/russia-economy-world-bank/index.html; Kramer, Andrew. September 19, 2014. "Russia Cuts Budget to Try to Spur Growth." *The New York Times*. www.nytimes.com/2013/09/20/business/global/russia-cuts-budget-to-try-to-spur-growth.html?_r=0.

[21] Events in Iraq in 2014, however, suggest a significant constraint on future supply growth, which could work in Russia's favor.

[22] Wilson, William T. May 19, 2014. "The Russian Economy Stares into the Abyss." Washington, DC: Heritage Foundation. www.heritage.org/research/reports/2014/05/the-russian-economy-stares-into-the-abyss.

[23] The Russian government moved to reduce the national budget in 2013 (including a freeze on military salaries and a reduction in retiree pension funds), reflecting an expectation of lower revenues and slower economic growth in 2014 and 2015. Kramer, Andrew. September 19, 2014. "Russia Cuts Budget to Try to Spur Growth." *The New York Times*. www.nytimes.com/2013/09/20/business/global/russia-cuts-budget-to-try-to-spur-growth.html?_r=0.

[24] Burbulis, Gennady, and Michele Berdy. June 20, 2011. "Meltdown." *Foreign Policy*. www.foreignpolicy.com/articles/2011/06/20/meltdown; Conway, Patrick. June 1995. "Currency Proliferation: The Monetary Legacy of the Soviet Union." *Essays in International Finance*, No. 197. www.princeton.edu/~ies/IES_Essays/E197.pdf.

[25] Pismennaya, Evgenia, and Olga Tanas. June 10, 2014. "Why Putin Raiding Wealth Fund Won't Cure What Ails Russia." *Bloomberg*. www.bloomberg.com/news/2014-07-10/why-putin-raiding-wealth-fund-won-t-cure-what-ails-russia.html.

[26] Ghosh, Palash. January, 22, 2014. "Putin Regime Could Fall If Oil Price Drops To $60." *International Business Times*. www.ibtimes.com/putin-regime-could-fall-if-oil-price-drops-60-fund-manager-browder-1545877.

[27] Cohen, Ariel. March 28, 2012. "A Threat to the West: The Rise of Islamist Insurgency in the Northern Caucasus and Russia's Inadequate Response." Washington, DC: The Heritage Foundation. www.heritage.org/research/reports/2012/03/a-threat-to-the-west-the-rise-of-islamist-insurgency-in-the-northern-caucasus.

[28] United Nations. "Human Development Index Trends, 1980-2013." UNDP. hdr.undp.org/en/content/table-2-human-development-index-trends-1980-2013.

[29] In its *Golden Rules for a Golden Age of Gas*, the IEA predicts that under the most favorable circumstances, European shale production could help mitigate the expected decline in European gas production out to 2035; in its unfavorable case, the lack of shale production results in domestic European shale production declining by three-fifths. See IEA. May 29, 2012. "Table 3.6," Golden Rules for a Golden Age of Gas. p. 129. www.worldenergyoutlook.org/goldenrules/.

[30] Interview by author, New York, June 1, 2014.

[31] IEA, 2013 World Energy Outlook; BP, Energy Outlook 2035; Chow, Edward C., and Anne Hudson. November 20, 2013. "The Russia-EU Gas Relationship: A partnership of necessity." Washington, DC: Center for Strategic and International Studies. csis.org/publication/russia-eu-gas-relationship-partnership-necessity.

[32] A.T. Kearney. December 2011. *The Future of European Gas Supply*. www.atkearney.com/paper/-/asset_publisher/dVxv4Hz2h8bS/content/the-future-of-the-european-gas-supply/10192.

Part 4

CHAPTER 6

Advice for the Obama Administration on Putin, Russia, and Ukraine

John Beyrle
Board Member
U.S. Russia Foundation

CHAPTER 7

Russia and the United States' National Interest (Or Reset Version 2.0)

Stephen Biegun
Vice President
Ford Motor Company
Board Member
U.S. Russia Foundation

CHAPTER 8

Russia, the Ukraine Crisis, and American National Interests

Graham Allison
Director, Belfer Center for Science and International Affairs
Harvard University

CHAPTER 9

Concluding Observations:
What We Heard

Stephen Hadley
Principal
RiceHadleyGates, LLC

"With the threat—if not the full decimating reality—of EU and U.S. sanctions now fully on display, the ideal time has come for Western leaders to discuss and agree on a strategy of engagement with the Kremlin, and with Kyiv, to make use of the leverage that sanctions have provided for the most effective use of diplomacy."

—JOHN BEYRLE

Advice for the Obama Administration on Putin, Russia, and Ukraine

John Beyrle
Board Member
U.S. Russia Foundation

The start of the Obama presidency in 2009 was marked by many a hopeful beginning, but perhaps none with such high stakes as the effort to forge a different kind of relationship with Russia. I was fortunate that my time as ambassador in Moscow coincided with a dramatic improvement in relations between Washington and Moscow, as a result. In some ways, this "reset" was sudden and unexpected; in others, it was inevitable. For decades, U.S.-Russia relations have followed a cyclical, boom-or-bust model. In my experience, the problem with the upswings—whether we call them a reset, détente, or peaceful coexistence—is not that they fail to yield measurable improvements in our interactions with Moscow. Arms control treaties, joint space flight, and Russia's accession to the WTO are only the most conspicuous examples of these over the decades. The problem with "resets" is that they never last. And what follows them is almost inevitably a troubled period in which both sides question the utility and even the feasibility of a partnership between Russia and the West. In the wake of Russia's annexation of Crimea and continued aggression against Ukraine, clearly we have again arrived at such a point.

America's most vital, even existential interests dictate that a constructive, productive relationship with Moscow is worth the extraordinary effort that seems necessary to achieve it. The still-unanswered question remains whether such a relationship is possible. When President Obama spoke to graduates of the New Economic School during his visit to Moscow in June 2010, he made a simple declaration—*America wants a strong, peaceful, and prosperous Russia*—in words that echoed similar statements by his three immediate predecessors. Nothing that has happened in the intervening four years has changed this fundamental assertion of American interests. What has changed, though, is the willingness of Russia's leaders to accept that the U.S. and the West are committed to that goal, part of President Putin's espousal of a worldview for Russia that rejects the West as a model or a mentor. For Putin, this is far from a novel departure. When I arrived in Moscow as ambassador in July 2008, I found the relationship as dangerously frayed as I had ever seen it—a consequence of Russia's turn away from the West that began during Putin's first term and was expressed most dramatically in his 2007 speech at the Munich security conference. It had many causes, including the expansion of NATO, the bombing of Serbia, and the perceived unilateralism of the U.S. war in Iraq. But the main factor underlying all of this was economic. The oil-and-gas-funded reversal of fortune that began after 2002 had convinced the Russian power elite that they really didn't need the West. Moreover, a belief took hold that the West in general and the U.S. in particular were ignoring or infringing on Russia's interests, fueling a sense of grievance best captured in the Russian adjective *obidcheviy*, describing a person spoiling for a fight who looks for slights and insults in order to take umbrage. The 2008 war with Georgia was an acute manifestation of this neurosis, with exaggerated narratives of American support for Saakashvili aggravating the injury and making the foe seem as much Washington as Tbilisi.

With things at this dismally low ebb, there was almost nowhere to go but up. In light of the current crisis over Ukraine, which represents an even greater level of rancor and discord, it is worth examining how and why the reset was possible. Most obviously, the election of a new administration in Washington—which could not be blamed for the perceived sins of the outgoing one—made it easier for Moscow to turn a new page. It is now also increasingly evident that Dmitry Medvedev, while never an independent or unfettered actor as president, was nonetheless granted significant latitude to develop a more constructive relationship with Washington. But once again, the principal motivating factor enabling the reset was economic. The global recession hit Russia harder than any other emerging economy, piercing the myth that Russia's prosperity was independent of and impervious to external shocks. Falling energy prices caused GDP to drop over 10 percent, pushing Russia's budget suddenly and deeply into deficit and reviving memories of default from 1998 that were still vivid to everyone in the Russian leadership. This, in turn, provided ammunition to economic reformers inside the government who had long argued that only modernization and diversification of Russia's hydrocarbon-based economy could make the country more globally competitive.

This was the silver lining of the 2008–2010 economic downturn: it produced broad consensus across the elite, including oligarchs with substantial stakes in state-controlled enterprises like Russian Railways, Rosneft, and even Gazprom, that the country's economic model was unsustainable and needed a big infusion of capital and know-how—and preferably from the West, not China or Japan. This was not so different from other periods of Russian history when the leadership had been forced to confront the reality of how far Russia lagged behind. The innovation entrepreneurs that Russia courted in Silicon Valley and paid handsomely to help launch Skolkovo and other innovation corridors are descendants of the Dutch shipbuilders that Peter the Great brought in to build his navy, or the truck assembly lines that Stalin imported from Detroit in the 1930s. (A new and significant aspect was how this instinct spread to the military, which began paying a premium to buy modern systems from abroad: the French Mistral, Israeli UAVs, and Italian ACVs.)

All of this, though, amounted only to a tactical tilt in our direction, a temporary effort to help Russia close the gap and redress its backwardness through a quick injection of capital and technology. It clearly did not constitute a strategic reassessment or realignment of Russia's worldview. Over that elemental question—Where does Russia belong?—the internal debate continues much as it has for centuries, dominated by two competing schools of thought. One camp sees Russia's identity and success tied up in closer association, and now economic integration, with the West, meaning Europe and North America. A second, conservative group, dominated by leaders of the security and military services, views the outside world with suspicion and hostility and longs to recapture Russia's lost imperial might. Both groups are united by the goal of ensuring Russia is accorded the status of a great global power, but they differ sharply on the tactics to achieve it. For the latter, statist camp ("imperial nostalgics," as Zbigniew Brzezinski dubbed them), a new Moscow-centric Eurasian Union must be created as a counterweight to the EU and NATO. For the modernizers, Russia's accession to the WTO was seen as a powerful tool to force a fight against the corruption and inefficiencies that hamstring Russia's competitiveness, and thus hinder her great power ambitions.

Putin's sympathies naturally favor the conservative camp, a consequence of his training and experience in the KGB and FSB. Russia's anti-Western policies since his return to the Kremlin in 2012 are a continuation and sharpening of the course he began to set during his first two terms. But Putin is not an ideologue. Alongside his aggressive and often emotional behavior, he has often shown a strong streak of pragmatism regarding what he views as core Russian interests. One week after the 9/11 attacks, he overruled his closest security advisers (including several who are now inside the small group discussing Ukraine) and gave the green light for U.S. force deployments in Central Asia. Despite continued calls for reciprocal moves to respond to U.S. economic sanctions and visa bans, Putin has refused to consider action in the two areas where America is most dependent on Russian cooperation: military transit to and from Afghanistan via the Northern Distribution Network and ferrying U.S. astronauts to the International Space Station. A top aide to President Putin told me recently that those two areas were probably "off limits." The same adviser predicted the Russian side would not move to restrict economic cooperation with the U.S. or Europe. Despite the bravado of Russian statements that economic sanctions will only end up making Russia less reliant on the West, Putin respects the arguments of Alexei Kudrin and others in the economic modernization camp that Russia's economic fortunes in the short to medium term depend on access to capital and investment from the West.

Much has been made of Russia's "pivot to China" as an alternative market and economic partner. Among the Russian business elite, though, Putin's meeting with President Xi after the annexation of Crimea was seen less as an epochal shift and more as a shrewd tactical move designed to make a necessity (stronger economic / energy links with China) look more like a choice (rebalancing away from the West). On the surface, it looked like a strong play, but a number of Russians I spoke with in Moscow recently, including MPs and key oligarchs, sounded worried that it amounts to Russia ceding too much control to the Chinese. In this view, Putin's aggression in Ukraine is drying up the loans and investment from the West that were counted on to plug the deficit over the next two to three years. When relations with the West were productive, Putin's bargaining position with Beijing was stronger. Now the Chinese see him as needy and have made clear they intend to get what they want for the prices they set. In the end, the prospect of dependence on China worries the Russian elite, and doubtless Putin himself, much more than dependence on the West.

The scale of the commercial and financial interdependence that has grown between Russia and the West, along with the clear disinclination for active military intervention by Western powers, has made economic sanctions seem a logical and powerful tool to compel Russia to abandon its effort to control the future of eastern Ukraine. But like military action itself, economic sanctions are necessary but not sufficient in and of themselves, unless the ultimate goal is destruction or serious disabling of Russia's economy. It is the threat of serious economic consequences backing up a parallel, active effort to encourage a negotiated resolution of the disputes between Moscow and Kyiv that is likely to have the greatest chance of changing the dysfunctional dynamics at work in the Ukraine crisis.

In the current atmosphere of anti-Western bravado, continued resort to sanctions could reach a point of diminished returns, strengthening the hand of the conservative forces who are the most hostile to the West and whose strongest arguments to Putin depend on the ability to demonstrate that U.S. and EU hostility toward Russia is greater than the West's own economic interests—an update of Lenin's famous bromide about capitalists and the sale of rope. It plays directly into their advocacy of a more independent, statist mode of development and provides evidence that reliance on Western trade, investment, and credits is a direct threat to Russia's existential interests. (From their own peculiar perspective, of course, they have a point—much of the positive evolution in the Russian business and investment climate over the past 15–20 years came from importing the best practices of Western corporate culture, which is a direct threat to corruption and cronyism.) Western sanctions also allow Putin to redirect popular dissatisfaction over the stagnant economic performance away from its true root causes—corruption and failure to modernize and diversify—and blame it on Washington, an accusation guaranteed to resonate with the 65 percent of Russians who consistently tell pollsters they view the United States government as unfriendly or hostile.

There are reasonable grounds for debate over whether the sanctions that have been implemented, including the latest round of "phase three" sectoral sanctions announced by the U.S. and EU, will have a measurable effect on the Russian economy, which would compel Putin to direct the Russian military and security services to cease supporting the separatists in eastern Ukraine. While it seems clear that the actions taken to date have had a chilling effect on the investment climate and provoked a flood of capital outflow—now running at two to three times the rate for 2013— there is less agreement that this in and of itself can be enough of a coercive factor to cause Putin to change course. Mikhail Khodorkovsky and others assess that Russia's fiscal reserves and the peculiarities of the energy distribution system will insulate the Russian economy from any serious damage for three to five years. The message Putin delivered to his assembled Security Council and the Russian people after the Malaysian plane was shot down amounted to two unambiguous assertions: Russia is a strong power, and we will not be forced to act against our will and our interests.

What has until now been missing in the Western effort to change Russia's course is direct dialogue with its principal architects. Some have argued that Putin's anti-Western rhetoric, and his criticism of "liberal Western values" as inimical to Russia's Slavic orthodox conservatism, means that he no longer cares whether the West approves of his actions or not. But those who know Putin warn against underestimating the degree to which he has been affected by things like Russia's suspension from the G-8 and the "shunning effort" undertaken by Obama, Merkel, and Cameron. In private conversations, several people close to the inner circle have described Putin's genuine irritation over the refusal of Western leaders to engage in face-to-face dialogue with him in any meaningful way. As one put it, "phone calls [alone] will not do the job." With the threat—if not the full decimating reality—of EU and U.S. sanctions now fully on display, the ideal time has come for Western leaders to discuss and agree on a strategy of engagement with the Kremlin, and with Kyiv, to make use of the leverage that sanctions have provided for the most effective use of diplomacy.

By far the least likely outcome, and the riskiest approach, is assuming that sanctions have begun to fracture Putin's base of support among the Russian elite. The transition from Putin to a successor will require a complicated series of negotiations among the clans that have grown fantastically wealthy and powerful during his reign and who will demand total assurance that their fortunes, families, and personal fates will be guaranteed in any transfer of power. The difficulty inherent in such a process—which Putin himself must initiate—makes it highly likely that he will put this off until late into his final term as president, 2018–2024. The degree of sanctions-related economic disruption needed to accelerate that timetable would bring with it a high risk of unintended consequences, including an even more brutal level of military adventurism.

So, like it or not, we need to face the high probability that we will be dealing with Vladimir Putin as the ultimate decider in the Kremlin into the next decade. And Putin and the small circle around him, whether they like it or not, must recognize that they cannot will themselves out of economic interdependence with the West—the lesson of 1998 and 2009, now being reinforced by the latest drop in Russian economic growth. We may well now be at a moment of maximum leverage, and the Obama administration should seize the initiative and enlist European support for a high-level and sustained diplomatic effort involving the U.S., EU, Russia, and Ukraine to negotiate an end to the fighting and set in place a process leading to more normal relations between Moscow and Kyiv.

John Beyrle served as an American diplomat for more than three decades, in foreign postings and domestic assignments focused on Central and Eastern Europe, the Soviet Union, and Russia. He was twice appointed ambassador: to Bulgaria (2005-08) and to Russia (2008-12). Ambassador Beyrle's diplomatic service included two earlier tours at the U.S. Embassy in Moscow, including as Deputy Chief of Mission. He also served as Counselor for Political and Economic Affairs at the U.S. Embassy in the Czech Republic and was a member of the U.S. Delegation to the CFE Arms Control Negotiations in Vienna. His Washington assignments included Special Adviser to the Secretary of State for the New Independent States, and Director for Russian, Ukrainian, and Eurasian Affairs on the staff of the National Security Council. Ambassador Beyrle has received the Presidential Distinguished Service Award from President Obama and the Presidential Meritorious Service Award from President George W. Bush. In April 2012 Secretary of State Clinton presented him with the State Department's highest honor, the Secretary's Distinguished Service Award. Retired from the Foreign Service in 2012, Ambassador Beyrle serves on the board of directors of several nonprofit organizations and investment firms. He speaks Bulgarian, Czech, French, German, and Russian.

"[U.S. policy toward Russia] must contend with the sobering reality of a relationship that has deteriorated dramatically. It must also assume for the foreseeable future a Russian government that is hostile, nationalistic, and undemocratic. A fundamental objective of U.S. policy toward Russia should be to reverse this course."

—STEPHEN BIEGUN

Russia and the United States' National Interest (Or Reset Version 2.0)

Stephen Biegun
Vice President
Ford Motor Company
Board Member
U.S. Russia Foundation

In evaluating the United States' national interest with today's Russia and what strategies and policies might best be pursued to achieve our aims, it is perhaps useful to keep in mind Mark Twain's admonition that "history does not repeat itself, but it does rhyme." The debate over how we should understand the events in Russia, Ukraine, and beyond has been compactly explained through a form of rhyme—the use of historical analogies.

For example, there are some who would attribute the growing authoritarianism of Vladimir Putin's Russia and the increasing instability in Central Europe to mostly be a reaction to mistaken Western policies similar to the *victors' justice* that emerged from the Treaty of Versailles at the end of World War I. Those who hold this view conflate the heavy war reparations demanded from Germany in that era with heavy handed and mistaken Western aid to Russia after the collapse of the Soviet Union (i.e., efforts to force Russia to become like us). By this thinking, and in the view of Russian nationalist myth, Western assistance was both intrusive and aimed at actually subverting Russian greatness (an argument superficially supported by the terrible economic distress of the immediate post-Soviet period). Likewise, the United States is faulted for an overly strong backing of the corrupt regime of President Boris Yeltsin, a perception that to this day among many in Russia arouses a deep and cynical resentment about the very notion of "democracy."

This analogy argues that the enlargement of NATO to Russia's borders in the 1990s confronted Russia not only with its own weakness, but also provoked a historically anchored, nationalistic fear of potential invasion from the West. Along with this, NATO is criticized for ignoring Russia's opposition to (and exploiting a weakened Russia's inability to prevent) the use of force to end Slobodan Milosevic's genocidal marauding in the former Yugoslavia. By the same token, the United States is seen to have failed in the last decade to reciprocate the magnanimity of President Putin in standing down while the U.S. military invaded and overthrew the Taliban regime and al Qaeda forces in Afghanistan in the aftermath of 9/11. Finally, many who hold this view find the West particularly guilty of not understanding the historic Russian character of the Crimean Peninsula (and by definition Russia's proper claims to the territory), especially when juxtaposed against what is seen as hypocritical Western support for Kosovar independence from Serbia.

Others see in the conduct of contemporary Russia a sequence of steps similar to those that played out in Germany and its neighboring lands during the 1930s—a defeated nation choosing a new leader through a quasi-democratic election followed by his consolidation of power into an authoritarian and even dictatorial regime; an aggrieved population on the losing side of history having its nationalist appetite fueled by a unscrupulous government with a propagandistic state-controlled media; a society in which all signs of dissent are met by the crushing power of the state; and ultimately the use of expansionist power to right historical wrongs (including territorial) and deliver national renaissance and greatness.

This analogy draws upon an abundant offering from the pre-World War II years, including Adolf Hitler's democratic election as the leader of Germany, the *Anschluss* (Austria's incorporation into Germany on the eve of World War II), Germany's seizure of the Sudetenland (the ethnically German territories that were attached to Czechoslovakia in the aftermath of World War I), and even the very rhetoric and word constructs used by President Vladimir Putin (most clearly in his tour de horizon celebrating the seizure of Crimea before the Russian Federal Assembly).

Finally, and not mutually exclusive of either of the previous two historical analogies, there are many who have reached the conclusion that Russia and the West have embarked upon a new Cold War. By this thinking, Russia may well be seeking to re-create, at least in geography and political control, as much of the former Soviet Union as possible. And, by extension, the Russian regime and even contemporary Russian society are destined to be in conflict with the West.

Are any of these analogies true, or mostly true? And if so, what should U.S. policies be in response? If the turn for the worse by Vladimir Putin's Russia is truly a result of our own heavy-handedness and lack of respect, should we tone down our concerns about the development of Russia's internal liberties and redouble efforts to find constructive areas of engagement and mutual cooperation? If we are witnessing the early days of the rise of a globally threatening regime, backed by a powerful military and bent on restoring its national glory through the seizure of territory, should we respond much more forcefully than our European forebears initially did 80 years ago? And, if we are embarking upon a new Cold War, should we isolate the Russian government, cut off U.S.-Russian commerce, and pursue Cold War era *real politik* in our relationships with potential partners in Europe, the Middle East, and Asia? The answer to all of the above questions is the same: no.

Analogy is not without its place in evaluating policy choices, but as much as it can draw upon the lessons of history, policy should not be overly dependent upon it either. As important as it is to understand history, it can also bind policymakers into overly narrow or hasty judgments, leading to policies that provoke outcomes that are seen as least desirable. Despite the familiarity that analogy provides, contemporary judgments are nearly impossible to make with any degree of confidence, even with the benefit of a deep knowledge of history.

To this point, policy that is overly dependent on history can ignore the fact that every new crisis and challenge has unique attributes driven by the personalities, conditions, and choices of the day. A deep foreboding has been generated by the foreign and domestic policies of the Putin government in Russia. Yet, how do we judge what Russia is today? Those who travel frequently to Russia for government or business reasons or as simple tourists will almost universally challenge the notion that a monolith called Russia is hurtling uncontrollably toward a deeper and more threatening hostility against the West. In fact, it could be argued that despite the Russian government's slide toward authoritarianism, the Russian people today enjoy a level of freedom unprecedented in their entire thousand-year history as a people— freedom to access a full range of information and opinion, to prosper, to travel, and even to disagree with their government (albeit much more so within the confines of their homes than in the public commons). At the same time, there is also ample evidence to argue that Russian government and security institutions represent a threatening power, resting on the foundation of a corrupt economy, and using force to undermine and dominate neighbors while oppressing its own people.

In addressing the challenges that are emerging from Russia today, it is critical to first gain an understanding of several conditions that are simultaneously occurring— an increasingly authoritarian government, a kleptocratic circle of regime supporters and a growing societal nationalism combined with a relatively free people, and a deepening economic engagement with the outside world. As U.S. policymakers reach out to an old set of policy tools—isolations, sanctions, etc.—to address our interests with Russia, care must be taken not to overlook opportunities in today's Russia that can be leveraged to encourage the Russian government to move in a more constructive direction.

Consider that in the course of just two years, the United States government has lurched from a policy of "reset," which seemingly ignored most of the worrisome developments in Russia, to an escalating ladder of policy reminiscent of U.S. policies in Northeast Asia during the run-up to World War II (to use a historical analogy!). The dizzying sequence of events over the past six months has left U.S.-Russian relations today in a worse state than at any time since the early 1980s.

It would be unfair to blame this outcome entirely or even preponderantly on the United States, but what choices or policies might the U.S. or Europe have made that could have influenced the Russian government to take an alternative course, or limited the choices that the Russian government has made to the consternation of the West? Should we have been more openly critical of the Russian government's slide toward authoritarianism? Should we have been more diligent in exposing and containing the corruption and criminality of the Russian economy? Should the Russian government have paid a higher price for the invasion of Georgia? The answer to all of these questions is the same: yes.

While there is little doubt that the policies supported by President Vladimir Putin's regime are at best deeply undesirable and at worst highly dangerous to global peace and stability, there is ample room for debate on the choices before today's Western policymakers. For example, should we condition future cooperation with Russia upon the demand that Russia fully relinquish its sovereign claim to Crimea? Does Western investment and trade create greater openness and interdependence in Russia, or does it simply fill the coffers of the Russian economy in a manner that finances nationalist, irredentist ambitions? Should the U.S. and NATO redouble their commitment to the cause of enlargement to include new members like Georgia, Ukraine, or Moldova, or should a clear message be sent to Moscow that those ambitions are on hold? Should the United States and Europe isolate the Russian government or engage it more broadly? Is Russia by historical experience and national character doomed to play the role of an undemocratic adversary to the liberal democracies of the West? While each of these questions is of sufficient size for a lengthy consideration, the most pressing and important question is what is most in the United States' national interest to effectuate a better outcome with and within Russia today?

In the wake of the events in Ukraine, the Obama administration has embarked upon a comprehensive policy review of the U.S. approach to Russia, the first since the policy of *reset* was crafted in 2009. While probably at least two years late, this review nonetheless gives the current administration the opportunity to catch up to the reality of what has been happening inside Russia as well as in the Russian government's conduct in international affairs.

Clearly, the most urgent policy issue before the Obama administration is to address the crisis in Ukraine. It is in the United States' national interest to ensure Ukraine's ability to maintain its territorial integrity, and that the rebellion in eastern Ukraine is turned back as quickly as possible. If the Russian government's irredentist policies are ultimately successful in Ukraine, as they already have been in Moldova and Georgia, the security of several of Russia's other neighbors, particularly those with sizeable ethnic Russian populations, will be at risk. This in turn sets the stage for an even wider conflict that potentially could impact NATO members with Article 5 of the North Atlantic Treaty (mutual defense commitments from the NATO allies).

It is by now clear that whatever reactionary decision making and grasping at opportunity drove the Russian government's seizure of Crimea after the Ukrainian government was overthrown in Kiev in February 2014, Russia has embarked upon a concerted strategy of destabilization and control in ethnically populated areas of southern and eastern Ukraine. Russian advisors, possibly Russian soldiers, sophisticated Russian weapons, and cross-border support from the Russian military are all deployed against the Ukrainian forces seeking to reassert Kiev's control of those territories. The United States faces several layers of challenges in trying to help the Ukrainian government succeed.

In Ukraine, the U.S. must engage with a newly elected Ukrainian government that, with the recent resignation of the prime minister, is still in transition. Ukraine has only a weak and poorly trained military force at its disposal to attempt to bring order to its border areas with Russia, and the Ukrainian economy is weaker still. In Russia, the United States has a growing adversarial relationship with President Putin and his government, a relationship in which Putin is only strengthened politically by being more aggressive in Ukraine or more antagonistic with the United States. In Central and Eastern Europe, the United States has allies who nervously watch Russian behavior in Ukraine, seeking reassurance from the United States and NATO that Russian behavior will be stopped lest it later move on to their neighborhoods. In Europe, the United States finds itself with a divided EU that runs the gamut from seeking greater confrontation and punishment of Russia to outright indifference and appeasement. And, in the midst of all the turmoil in Europe, the United States continues to engage with EU partners and Russia in trying to respond to current crises in Israel, Syria, Iraq, and increasingly Afghanistan.

Looking at the Ukrainian crisis from the perspective of triage, the first and critical need is for the United States and its allies in Europe to help Ukraine bring an end to the fighting as quickly as possible. The longer the fighting goes on, the more civilian and military casualties there will be, and the deeper and more permanent the antagonism between the Russian and Ukrainian governments and their populations. Of course, this is easier said than done.

It is clear that if Ukraine is to retain its territorial integrity, and if the separatist rebellion is to be put down, Ukraine will need the right balance of increased military capabilities and decreased support for the separatists, combined with a convincing outreach to the now war-scarred and skeptical (if not hostile) ethnic Russian population of Ukraine. The U.S. and EU governments have sought to dissuade the Russian government from continued support for the separatists through escalating targeted and sectoral sanctions. As the aggression from Russia toward Ukraine has grown, so too have the consequences for the Russian economy. While sanctions to date have caused a deterioration of the Russian economy, they have not yet irreparably severed trade and investor relations between U.S. and EU companies and Russian partners and investors. In fact, uncharacteristically, the Russian government has not to date retaliated with reciprocal sanctions against non-Russian economies, perhaps aware that this would only bring greater harm to the Russian economy.

To bring the quickest possible end to the fighting in Ukraine, the United States and EU nations must provide all necessary assistance to improve the training and equipment of the Ukrainian forces. At a minimum this should take the form of the non-lethal aid that is already being delivered (uniforms, rations, night vision equipment, etc.). Additionally, Ukrainian forces should be provided real-time intelligence information that permits Ukrainian forces to most effectively target separatist forces, though questions persist about the reliability and ability of the Ukrainian military to make use of shared intelligence. Finally, if the Ukrainian military is lacking in the equipment necessary to fully defend its sovereign territory, the United States and European governments should assist the Ukrainian government in acquiring the military equipment necessary to improve its military effectiveness. Simply put, Ukraine is an independent nation with a democratically elected government seeking to defend its sovereignty against an externally driven military insurgency. In 21st century Europe, it is hard to see how not helping Ukraine defend its territorial integrity will do anything but come back to haunt us.

Without a doubt the direct provision of lethal assistance to the Ukrainian military comes at some risk. With the fighting happening in the midst of civilian populations, there remains a high risk of civilian casualties. Because of the proximity of the Russian border to the conflict, Ukrainian forces could also mistakenly fire on targets located within Russia. Poorly trained Ukrainian forces also would constantly be at some risk for battlefield loss, surrender, or diversion of weapons to separatist fighters. Most considerable is the degree to which this assistance provokes increased Russian military aid to the separatist forces—or even direct Russian military engagement in the conflict. It does not take much to imagine a scenario where, at a minimum, a proxy battle plays out between the respective allies of Russia and the West, if not direct fighting between a Western-supplied Ukrainian military against Russian regular forces. But, the alternative is to leave Ukrainian forces at a significant disadvantage whereby separatists are continuously supplied from across the Russian border along with rear echelon support, including intelligence, air defense, and artillery support.

Aside from increased military aid to the Ukrainian military, the only other means to bring an end to the fighting is to broker a multilateral diplomatic agreement between the EU, U.S., Ukraine, Russia, and, to the extent that they are in any way separate from Russia, the separatists themselves. So far, such efforts have been fruitless largely due to the ulterior aims of Russia and the separatists to lock in control of the territory they hold—presumably for the foreseeable future. Having watched as the Russian government used similar tactics to produce so-called frozen conflicts in other contested areas of the former Soviet Union (Abkhazia, South Ossetia, and Transnistria) and having seen Crimea forcefully incorporated into Russia, the Ukrainian government cannot accept an agreement that simply holds in place separatist control of large swaths of the border regions with Russia.

As the Obama administration embarks upon a review of policy toward Russia, larger consideration must be given to how to begin to change over time the nature of the U.S.-Russian relationship in order to produce a more constructive future.

This policy must contend with the sobering reality of a relationship that has deteriorated dramatically. It must also assume for the foreseeable future a Russian government that is hostile, nationalistic, and undemocratic. A fundamental objective of U.S. policy toward Russia should be to reverse this course.

Due to Russia's size, geography, resources, and role in international organizations, it is imperative for the United States to find some basis for a positive bilateral relationship with Russia regardless of the nature of Russia's governing regime. The goals of the new administration's Russia policy should be to encourage and nurture political liberalization inside Russia, to join with Russia as a friend and partner in expanding commerce and addressing various policy challenges of mutual concern, and to find cooperative approaches to international security issues even when our national interests diverge. The Russian government, which uses tension in the U.S.-Russia relationship for domestic political gain, will not make this realignment in U.S. policy easy. Under no circumstances should the goal of U.S. policy be simply to have good relations with Russia for their own sake. A central principle of U.S. policy must be to promote and defend its security interests along with supporting its friends and allies despite pressure and provocative actions by Russia.

While a dramatic change in U.S. policy is absolutely necessary, a new policy approach toward Russia should be much more than a simple renunciation of reset—it must represent a far more substantive shift in the tone and conduct of American policy. The contours of this shift in policy should become self-evident as the administration systematically develops policy options that gradually begin to put internal and external pressure on the Russian government to change its direction and policies. To be successful, this policy shift will require resolve and determination on the part of the United States, close cooperation with our allies, and effective efforts to reach past the Russian government's machinations to directly communicate with the Russian people. This policy should rest upon a strategy that seeks to frustrate Russian misdeeds abroad while building unrelenting pressure for positive internal change in Russian policies and governance.

In contrast with the Cold War, when containment and confrontation were the principal tools available to U.S. policymakers, the United States has at its disposal a broad array of political, diplomatic, economic, and information tools that, if effectively applied, will discourage the Russian government and its leaders from pursuing policies that undermine peace and security. It remains very much in the U.S. national interest to support the development of a democratic and stable Russia, at peace with its neighbors and able to engage constructively in addressing global challenges.

Over the past two U.S. administrations, it became increasingly uncomfortable for the U.S. government to openly criticize the deterioration of personal liberties in Russia. On those occasions where criticisms were made, there were no consequences.

At the same time, Russian government reaction to criticism reached a level that was almost hysterical and was used by the Russian authorities to launch waves of crackdowns against political opponents, non-governmental organizations, Western funding inside Russia, and even average citizens lawfully expressing their opposition to the deterioration of freedoms and the subversion of democratic processes. It is in the United States' national interests to use its own voice as well as the weight of organizations such as the Organization for Security and Cooperation in Europe (OSCE) to clearly condemn the subversion of democracy in Russia.

Using diplomatic and economic pressure to deter Russian misbehavior in Ukraine should not be confused with isolating Russia. Isolating Russia—its government, economy, and society—would close off the most important opening the United States ultimately has to influence the direction of the Russian government. Those in Russia who are most interested in fomenting hostile relations with the United States are most empowered when the U.S. presence is least. Constructive and open dialogue at a governmental level, deeper trade and investment, and greater people-to-people contact will, at a minimum, preserve the opportunity to improve relations if or when events in Ukraine settle. In both official and non-governmental capacities, the U.S. government, the U.S. business community, and NGOs must all be encouraged and supported in engaging counterparts in Russia to the maximum extent possible.

Maintaining a two-track policy of engagement and pressure will not be easy for U.S. policymakers. The United States should anticipate that Russian government provocations, both rhetorical and tangible, will continue as Moscow finds opportunities to challenge this shift in U.S. policy. While the United States and its allies are likely to be tested by these provocations, it would be beneficial to avoid being baited into reciprocal recriminations that lend support to the perception that U.S. hardliners and Russian hardliners are pursuing a Cold War redux. Instead, a new policy direction, and, where needed, pushback against these anticipated moves, should be central to the new U.S. strategic approach that through a measured voice subjects the Russian government to criticism for its disruptive policies. This policy should impose diplomatic and economic costs to Russian interests whenever Moscow pursues policies that threaten U.S. interests and weaken international peace and security.

In international affairs, the United States will be most successful in addressing challenges to its relationship with Russia when it supports and has the support of its friends and allies. In particular, the NATO Alliance and especially the Central and Eastern European nations offer an important point of engagement with Russia.

These states have experience with, are the closest to, and best understand what drives thinking in Moscow. Complemented by a strong call by the U.S. government for change inside Russia, efforts should be undertaken to amplify criticism and scrutiny of the corrupt and authoritarian actions that routinely characterize Russian government policies and actions.

A prominent objective of U.S. policy should be to promote transparency so that the international community is fully aware of Russian actions. The attention given to Russian-backed conflicts and ongoing Russian democratic and human rights abuses should be elevated, with strong American backing, in international and regional fora, such as the United Nations, the Arab League, and the OSCE. In short, the Russian government should find itself stretched thin and under the microscope for every abuse or destabilizing policy it pursues. This step, among many others, will help build the pressure to recalibrate Russian policies as Moscow begins to understand that the United States and its friends and allies can impose penalties when its actions undermine peace and security.

A major, complicating challenge in external relations with the Russian government is in the very nature of the Russian governing regime. Virtually every area of foreign policy concern that the United States has with the Russian government can be traced to two drivers—corruption and nationalism.

Russia is ruled by a mostly corrupt and self-serving set of elites who used the perversion of democratic processes to obtain power—and who continue to use non-democratic means to keep themselves in power. They are invested in the system financially and act in league with nationalistic security institutions that can oppress or repress internal dissent with impunity. These relatively few but powerful elites rely on collective collusion to function and are rarely vulnerable to internal divisions (almost always over the division of spoils rather than over matters of principle). Policies such as the Sergei Magnitsky Act, which targets individual human rights abusers for economic sanctions, are so vigorously opposed by the regime precisely because that law would identify and punish a handful of the corrupt elites who demand collective protection. These elites know instinctively that if they do not work together, their power and privileges likely will erode.

The regime in Moscow survives because it provides impunity to corrupt and wealthy oligarchs inside Russia, who it systematically rewards through control of valuable sectors of the economy, especially natural resources such as metals and hydrocarbons. In return, these corrupt and oligarchic interests provide loyalty and great wealth to the governing regime through bribery and payoffs. Whether because of fear, dependency on the government, or loyalty to the regime, there will be no quick reorientation of these wealthy interests in Russia. However, even without sanctions much more effort can be applied within the framework of existing laws and global agreements to present a more stark choice for those among Russia's wealthy who are also dependent upon access to the greater global economy. Global anti-corruption initiatives, close scrutiny of Russian trade competition (anti-monopoly) policies, and the active development of European alternatives to Russia's lucrative energy exports could put powerful economic pressure on Russia's governing structure to choose a different course or see their own interests decline.

The flip side of placing more pressure on Russian economic interests to conform to international legal norms is the ongoing importance of encouraging legitimate Western investment and trade with Russia. While there are exceptions to the rule, in general, Western trade and investment expose many Russians to the norms of law-based societies, invest them in a positive change in their country, and deepen interdependence between Russia and the outside world. In and of itself, this provides a form of pressure for the Russian government to conform to certain norms such as the World Trade Organization. But, in growing the size of the entrepreneurial and middle classes in Russia, a commensurate expansion of a political constituency has an incentive to support rule of law, transparency, and democratic influence over those who govern Russia. Western trade and investment will not be a panacea for all that ails Russia today, and it would be a huge overstatement to suggest that this alone will directly produce democracy. But an entrepreneurial business class more independent of government control in Russia is an important building block of a pluralistic society, which itself is the foundation upon which a stronger Russian democracy might be built.

The other major challenge to changing the nature of Russia's current government regime is the strong, nationalist bent that exists throughout Russian society. Despite international opprobrium and growing economic penalties, polling suggests that the vast majority of the Russian population still firmly backs the policies of President Putin. This nationalism, nurtured by the deterioration of independent media and the lack of a competitive political system, is aggravated and manipulated by corrupt elites who preserve their hold on power by demonizing potential opponents at home or abroad. The challenges that flow from this include threats to the independence of neighboring countries, the deterioration of democratic liberties and human rights in Russia, ongoing Russian support for pariah regimes (and corresponding commercial and military trade), and corruption at all levels in the Russian government and society.

To ease the growing divide between the Russian population and the West, it is important to redouble efforts to engage more closely with Russian society. Fully aware of the potential challenge that voices of dissent pose in Russia today, the Russian government has launched a smothering series of initiatives to prohibit, penalize, and prosecute the actions of non-governmental organizations within Russia. The NGO community has been severely restricted through the coercion of potential sources of funding within Russia, blocking of external sources of financing, branding of critics as foreign agents of foreign influence, and coercive policies aimed at limiting legal registration or public demonstrations by NGOs. With little or no fanfare, NGOs seeking to monitor and improve democratic and human rights in Russia should receive substantial U.S. financial support (which may have to occur outside of Russia only).

As a matter of the highest priority, a new policy toward Russia should connect directly to dissenting Russian citizens who, in bravely opposing the nature of the regime and its pathologies, are determined to bring about change. These people may be occasional protestors, or may be permanent members of the dissenting political class, or both. They march in the protests but have limited reach or influence over greater Russia. These are the natural friends and allies of a democratic future in Russia, but because of their criticism and their relationship with outside groups, Western institutions, and democratic governments, they are painted by the regime as anti-Russian, agents of foreign influence. The sobering reality is that the opposition in Russia is splintered, lacks popular support, and has been actively marginalized, discredited, and repressed by the Russian government. A particular challenge for the United States is to be supportive without seeming to co-opt or make more vulnerable those who are leading the efforts to liberalize Russia.

The ultimate success of a policy that seeks to build greater cooperation between the United States and Russian society rests upon the ability to connect to the middle of the Russian political system. These are the individuals who either benefit directly from the corruption, are intimidated from expressing any criticism of the system around them, or who simply seek to make a living to survive and prosper. These people do not rock the boat. However, this constituency has the influence and wherewithal to change Russia if they conclude that the current system poses greater risks than benefits to their vested interests.

The only way that the Russian government will ever move in a more moderate direction is if the Russian people themselves demand so. While the United States cannot and should not play any role in selecting who leads Russia, it is very much in the United States' interest to help create pressure and incentive inside Russia to change its government policies; at some point, the United States must help create the conditions that weaken the dependency of Russia's middle class on the whims of the current regime. This part of the political spectrum must see that the defense of what they have achieved (in some cases through often less than legal or honest means) is at great risk if the current regime's policies continue. A means must be found to shift their allegiances away from the corrupt authoritarianism of the current regime and toward a more transparent, rules-based, and democratic system that collectively will give them a greater say and certainty in how Russia is governed. In turning the page on the past, evolution toward the rule of law will also protect their ill-gotten gains behind a more dependable system that legitimizes and promotes democracy in Russia.

Perhaps the most difficult step will be to pursue policies that reach the rest of the Russian population, which is largely politically uninvolved. Men and women across that vast country who work to live, who try to separate themselves from the corruption around them (but occasionally fall in its path), and who, given a choice of working or marching, always choose working. They are manipulated by regime-controlled media, are generally not supportive of political dissidents, and are most likely to respond only when the stability of their lives and employment are threatened. For opponents of the current regime, the challenge is that the status quo is acceptable for this, the largest part of the Russian population. They even see the current political and economic situation as preferable to the chaos they personally experienced in the more democratic times of the 1990s (pre-Putin).

The bulk of the Russian population suffer no illusions about the nature of their corrupt and undemocratic government, but they demand that their corrupt and undemocratic government keep the economy growing and pay for such basic benefits as pensions. The fundamental threat to the Russian government, however, is if the economy or state support should falter, it could quickly earn the ire of the Russian people. History has shown that if aroused, the masses can change the course of Russia. But, on a worrisome note, this population is also easily manipulated by state-directed media and, with a strong, nationalistic bent, could just as easily become a force that makes the regime even more nationalistic and hostile.

Finally, tone and words matter. As much as possible, official comments on Russia should be phrased in a manner that takes the side of the Russian people against a corrupt and venal elite. Corruption—a fact of life in today's Russia— is almost universally resented, even by many of its perpetrators. When criticizing Russian government behavior, special care should be taken to refer to the "Russian government" rather than "Russia" or "the Russians." At times, the tone should lament how badly Russia is governed, and at other times it should be stern in criticizing the Russian government's failure to meet its own commitments through its constitution, laws, and international agreements to govern democratically and with respect for fundamental human rights. It should also clearly outline the elements of a positive vision for U.S.-Russian relations.

Historical analogies can help us evaluate the choices before us, and they give us the confidence that comes from knowing the lessons of the past. They do not however provide us with a simple roadmap to fully understand current events or the policies that will most successfully carry the United States through challenges like the current tensions with Russia. In that respect, more helpful and more powerful than an understanding of history is an understanding of ourselves and of the principles that we know have served the United States since its very founding. At every turn we must promote peace, but, if necessary, we will be prepared to respond to aggression. We will actively support the spread of freedom and the democratic voice of free peoples. We will engage openly with other nations at every level of government, economy, and society because we are confident that the ideals that we hold true are universally attractive and ultimately will be the choice of others. This is what will guide us through the current tensions with Russia. This is the national interest.

Stephen E. Biegun is a corporate officer and vice president for International Governmental Affairs at Ford Motor Company since 2004. In this role for Ford, Mr. Biegun oversees all aspects of Ford's international governmental relations, including trade strategy and international political risk. Prior to joining Ford, he served as national security advisor to Senate Majority Leader, Senator Bill Frist, M.D., from 2003-2004. In this capacity, he provided analysis and strategic planning for the Senate's consideration of foreign policy, defense and intelligence matters, and international trade agreements. Before joining the staff of the Majority Leader, he worked in the White House from 2001-2003 as Executive Secretary of the National Security Council. Prior to joining the White House staff, he served for 14 years on the staffs of the Senate Committee on Foreign Relations and the House Foreign Affairs Committee as a foreign policy adviser to members of both the House of Representatives and the United States Senate. He is a member of the Council on Foreign Relations and the Aspen Strategy Group and is a member of the board of directors of FordSollers, LLC (Ford Motor Company's Russian Joint Venture), the US-Russia Investment Fund, the US-Russia Foundation for Economic Development and the Rule of Law, the US-Russia Business Council, and the Moscow School of Political Studies. Mr. Biegun graduated from the University of Michigan where he studied Political Science and Russian Language.

"When faced with a challenge like the Ukraine crisis, the first question most American policymakers ask is: What should we do? From a strategic perspective, diagnosis should precede prescription. Until policymakers can answer the question "What is happening?" with some understanding of the dynamics of the pathology or challenge, it is impossible to choose an intervention with confidence that it will make things better rather than worse."

—GRAHAM ALLISON

Russia, the Ukraine Crisis, and American National Interests

Graham Allison
Director, Belfer Center for Science and International Affairs
Harvard University

The organizers of the Aspen Strategy Group workshop asked me to address three specific questions:

- How should the U.S. balance its competing strategic interests with Russia in reacting to the Ukraine crisis?

- Should we limit our future strategic engagement with Ukraine (as well as Georgia) in NATO in order to preserve our long-term relationship with Russia?

- How can we disagree with Putin on Ukraine and yet keep the door open to work together on other critical issues—Iran, Afghanistan, North Korea?

Briefly (and provocatively) my answers are:

- Carefully—recognizing that from the perspective of American national interests, Russia matters much more than Ukraine. The harsh but realistic bottom line is that nothing that has happened in Ukraine recently, or that is likely to happen there, will significantly impact American *vital* national interests. As the Commission on American National Interests notes, vital national interests are conditions strictly necessary for the survival and well-being of the United States as a free nation with our fundamental institutions and values intact.[1] In contrast, many choices made by Vladimir Putin's Russia can directly impact America's survival and well-being.

- Yes: NATO should tell Ukraine and Georgia that they will not be members of NATO for as far as the eye can see. (And we should be thankful that when an American administration sought to do otherwise in 2005-2008, European colleagues prevented excessive risk taking.) We should welcome them as NATO partners and allow them to buy arms from, train with, and operate with NATO members in multi-national combat missions like Afghanistan. But admission to membership in NATO carries with it an iron-clad commitment by the U.S. and other members to regard an attack upon a member as if it were an attack on our homeland. Americans are not willing to commit ourselves to fight Russians over Russia's disputes with Ukraine or Georgia.[2]

- Thoughtfully—as we should do in all relations in international affairs.[3] Russia is and will remain for the foreseeable future a Putin-led, autocratic, resentful, retro-KGB bully that threatens an array of American interests. We must counter these threats by carefully crafted strategies designed for each—from deterrence of potential nuclear threats to economic sanctions that impose costs for aggression against Ukraine. Determined opposition to an adversarial Russia does not, however, preclude intimate cooperation in selective areas where we face a common challenge. Americans prefer clarity in black and white, sharp distinctions between friends and enemies. Such expectations will create increasing frustration in the world of international relations. However clumsy, concepts like "frenemies" or "coopetition" will become more familiar as we think about relations not only with Russia, but with China, Saudi Arabia, and others.

As this essay is submitted in October 2014, a ragged cease-fire in eastern Ukraine has provided a window for negotiations. Yet the Ukrainian crisis remains unresolved, and it is possible at this point to sketch an array of alternative futures. My assignment in this essay, however, is not to predict the future, but rather to locate what has happened in the framework of American national interests. I will therefore leave predictions to other chapters in this volume, after one final introductory note.

As the swirling images create the impression of a world that has spun out of control, it is tempting to see in Putin's KGB statecraft the makings of another Cold War. Americans like familiar story lines. If we were casting a movie, Putin would be tailor-made for the role of the villain viewers love to hate. At the same time, American domestic politics tilt toward Cold War II—even if, like many sequels, the latter version is a pale imitation of the original. Awakened from their slumber, some old Cold Warriors respond with enthusiasm to the prospect of renewed relevance.

Nevertheless, as Henry Kissinger has wisely counseled, "Demonization of Vladimir Putin is not a policy."

This paper will attempt to address the assigned questions from a strategic perspective. Part I provides a framework for strategic analysis. It has been developed in a course I have taught at Harvard over the past three decades (co-teachers have included Joe Nye, Bob Blackwill, and currently David Sanger). Part II uses that framework to analyze challenges posed by Russia today. Part III uses the framework to analyze challenges posed by Ukraine today. Part IV concludes with my assessment of the Obama administration's actions to date: what it has gotten wrong, what it has gotten right, and what should now be done.

Part I: Framework for analysis

When faced with a challenge like the Ukraine crisis, the first question most American policymakers ask is: What should we do? From a strategic perspective, diagnosis should precede prescription. Until policymakers can answer the question "What is happening?" with some understanding of the dynamics of the pathology or challenge, it is impossible to choose an intervention with confidence that it will make things better rather than worse. Because diagnosis is often difficult, Hippocrates' counsel "first, do no harm" became a central tenant in medicine. We can dream of the day when it becomes a truism in foreign policy as well.

The second question from a strategic perspective is: Why do we care? Specifically, what must the U.S. government care about *more* than other things that we care about? In a globalized world, everything is connected to everything. God cares about every sparrow. But governments cannot care equally about everything. Thus a *hierarchy* of national interests requires identifying core or vital interests that are essential in the oft-repeated mantra "to preserve the U.S. as a free nation with our fundamental institutions and values intact." In a nation's hierarchy of interests, core priorities are more important than other interests, which may not be unimportant, but are just not vital. While politicians and diplomats use the term "vital" promiscuously, analysts should follow the counsel of the Commission on American National Interests and restrict its use to the dictionary definition of the word: essential for survival and well-being.

Question three for a strategist is: What is our margin for impact? Washington conversations typically presume that the U.S. is the prime mover of whatever is happening. Discussions of strategy thus start, and too often stop, with the question: What is our objective? What do we want to achieve? Analytically, the vast majority of causal factors shaping events that pose challenges for us—for example, in Ukraine or Russia today—are not American actions. In Rick Warren's good line, "It's not about us." Statesmanship, as Bismarck observed, requires first listening carefully for the footsteps of God and then trying to leap up and grab his hem as he goes by.

Part II: Russia today

Using this framework, key questions about Russia are: What is the challenge? What are the key trend lines and drivers shaping events in Russia that can impact us? What should we care about most? And what are our margins for impact?

Before the current crisis in Ukraine, when the topic of Russia arose in most policy circles, the dominant response was a combination of fatigue and disgust, frequently followed by the refrain: Russia doesn't matter anymore. A word cloud from major press outlets over the past decade finds the most frequent adjectives include brutal, declining, corrupt, bully, and failing. Few will debate the fact that Russia is all of these and worse.

Nonetheless, if we locate recent developments on a larger historical canvas, the aftershocks of the Soviet empire's implosion have been relatively peaceful, at least to this point. When the Soviet Union collapsed, Russia's borders retreated to the era of Peter the Great. That trauma has left Russia's leadership, especially Putin and his narrow circle of former-KGB operatives, suffering from post-imperial stress disorder. In a word, Putin is PISD. But only in Georgia and Ukraine has Russia used force to adjust ragged borders.

Most observers have forgotten the priority worries about threats to America that would follow the collapse of what Ronald Reagan rightly called the "evil empire." Assessing the past two decades, we have much for which to give thanks. The Soviet Union's collapse left 3,200 strategic nuclear weapons in Ukraine, Kazakhstan, and Belarus, in addition to 14,000 tactical nuclear weapons in these and other newly independent states. This raised the specter of "loose nukes" that would find their ways into the hands of terrorists who would conduct a nuclear 9/11. But 23 years on, thanks to extraordinary cooperation between Russia's nuclear custodians and the U.S., not a single nuclear warhead has been found in the world's arms bazaars—or used. Surly, thuggish, and autocratic as it is, Putin's regime is not the "black hole" that Bob Gates warned the Aspen Strategy Group about in 1999. Nor is it an extreme version of the "authoritarian, nationalist, reflexively adversarial, and possibly revanchist Russia" that "in its virulent form, [this] would be a Weimar successor with a Russian accent" which then seemed another plausible future.[4]

The core question in thinking about Russia is: What must the U.S. government care about more than other things that it cares about? Briefly stated:[5]

- Despite the fact that it is Cold War detritus, the most inconvenient truth remains that Russia is the only nation that can by its own unilateral choice *erase the United States from the map.* As a consequence of technology, we are, in Churchill's metaphor, "Siamese twins." Even when the "evil empire" was our deadliest enemy, it was simultaneously our inescapable partner in avoiding the nuclear war in which we would both be the first victims.

- If Presidents Barack Obama and George W. Bush are correct in identifying *nuclear terrorism* as the single largest threat to American national security— and I believe they are—Russia is our most consequential partner in addressing that threat.

- Russia plays an essential role in preventing the *proliferation of nuclear weapons*, missile-delivery systems, and advanced weapons like the SA11 that shot down Malaysian Airlines MH17. In the current effort to prevent Iran from acquiring nuclear weapons, Russia's choices to sell—or withhold—key technologies (for example, S-300s or S-400s) make the difference between the possibility of success and almost certain failure. Without Russia, Syria's chemical weapons stockpile would not have been eliminated.

- Russia has been an active partner in *counterterrorism* intelligence sharing and even operations against Al Qaeda and other transnational terrorist groups. Since ISIL poses at least as great a threat to Russia as it does to the U.S., Russia could play a significant role in its defeat.

- Russia provided an essential *supply line* for American troops in Afghanistan, remains an important conduit for material exiting Afghanistan, and shares our interest in the stability of Afghanistan after U.S. withdrawal.

- Russia is the *world's largest exporter of hydrocarbons*: number one in gas and second only to Saudi Arabia in oil. Over the past decade, Russia has added more oil and gas to global energy markets than any other nation. Even if in the next decade North America becomes "energy self-sufficient," it will never be independent of global energy prices. Russian supplies will have a major impact on those prices. Russia is and will remain for many years the key supplier of gas to Germany, Italy, and most of Europe.

- It is no accident that Russia is one of the five veto-wielding *permanent members of the UN Security Council* and a member of the G20 (even if currently excluded from the G8). In the strategic triangle with China, a Moscow more closely aligned with the U.S. would be significant in shaping a balance of power in which China can emerge as a global power without overturning the existing order. Conversely, the thickening alignment between Russia and China provides a counter-balance to the U.S. and its Western allies and emboldens China's assertiveness in Asia.

- As the *largest country* on earth by land area—abutting China in the east, Poland in the west, and the U.S. across the Bering Strait—Russian territory provides transit corridors for supplies to global markets whose stability is vital to the U.S. economy.

- Russia's potential as a *spoiler* in international affairs is difficult to exaggerate. Consider what a Russian president intent on frustrating U.S. international objectives could do. There can be no doubt that Russia has many options, from fracturing the P5+1 negotiating process with Iran by selling advanced air defenses to Tehran or collapsing the Iran sanctions regime (through a major trade of oil for goods or nuclear reactors) to supporting Chinese territorial claims in its near abroad.

In relations with Putin's Russia, the results of the Obama administration's balancing act remain to be seen. Initially it vilified Putin and indicted Russia's "19th century" behavior that posed a "threat to the established international order." At the same time, however, President Obama was clearly working behind the scenes to awaken feckless European allies, engaging Chancellor Angela Merkel to coordinate a package of sanctions that significantly raise the costs for Russia. Moreover, he has resisted political pressure from Democrats as well as Republicans to declare Cold War II. In announcing the most recent sanctions, Obama argued specifically this is "not a new Cold War." Instead, in his terms, "it is a very specific issue related to Russia's unwillingness to recognize that Ukraine can chart its own path." Furthermore, he has stretched to leave space for a resolution that would allow selective cooperation. While there is no prospect that U.S. relations with Putin's Russia will return to the pre-Ukraine hope for a predominately cooperative partnership, both nations have continued selective cooperation to implement nuclear arms control treaties, counter Iran's nuclear ambitions, eliminate Assad's declared stockpile of chemical weapons, and reduce risks that nuclear weapons or materials fall into the hands of terrorists.

In the longer run, the forces of globalization and modernization will have a powerful magnetic pull, especially with the emergent educated middle classes of Russia. But for the year ahead, analyzing the sticks and carrots the U.S. and Europe are able and willing to apply in response to the Ukraine crisis versus those available to Putin's Russia, my assessment is that Russia has both higher stakes and higher cards than does the West and that this reality will be reflected in whatever solution emerges.

Part III: Ukraine

Much of the debate about what the U.S. should do in response to developments in Ukraine underlines the need to remember Hippocrates's first principle. (To emphasize this point, in my course at Harvard, before recommending a treatment, students are required to take a quiz about the patient. About Ukraine, for example, I asked: before Khrushchev transferred Crimea to Ukraine in 1954, in which century had Crimea been part of Ukraine? When they fail the quiz, I have been known to ask them: If they were the patient, and the doctor were unable to provide satisfactory answers to analogous questions about their illness, would they be willing to let him perform surgery on them?[6])

Ukraine's most pressing challenges include:

- A flailing, *nearly failing state*: a decade ago, today, and most likely a decade hence.

- A *population sharply* divided in identity and aspirations between West and East (with many further divisions within each). Ethnic Russians—who mostly reside in the southeast—constitute at least a quarter of Ukraine's population. Opinion polls consistently show they favor greater ties with Russia, whereas western Ukrainians favor integration into the European Union and NATO.

- *Oligarchic ownership* of wealth, economic production, and seats in parliament. The 100 richest Ukrainians control two-thirds of the country's GDP. The country's billionaires boast openly about "owning" Ukrainian MPs and exercise tight control of key factions in the Rada.

- Financially bankrupt *failing economy* (having amassed a national debt of $75 billion, which amounts to more than half of Ukraine's GDP, and requires $35 billion in the next two years to avoid default).

- Extreme *dependence on Russia*: for 60 percent of its gas, one-third of imports, and one-third of exports. Remittances from Ukrainians working in Russia accounted for 12 percent of Ukraine's GDP last year.

- *Dependence on the IMF* to avoid immediate default—but with a current bailout subject to standard IMF conditions (requiring elimination of subsidies that are unlikely to be implemented, raising the prospect that this becomes the third failed IMF bailout of Ukraine).[7]

From the perspective of American national interests, the most important good news is that Ukraine has no nukes. Imagine recent events with nuclear warheads atop

ICBMs aimed at American cities that stood alert on Ukrainian soil in 1993. Indeed, in 2012 at the Seoul Nuclear Security Summit, Ukrainian President Viktor Yanukovych stood up to announce that the last 15 bombs' worth of highly enriched uranium that had been in Kharkiv and Sevastopol had been eliminated. Had that material not been eliminated, the U.S. would now face a qualitatively different problem.[8]

A second point of good news—from the perspective of the U.S.—is that Ukraine is not a member of NATO. That means that the U.S. does not have an Article 5 commitment to respond to an attack upon Ukraine as an attack upon us. Imagine that Ukraine had been admitted to NATO (as the Bush administration tried to do) and that Putin had reacted as he did to the prospective loss of its naval base at Sevastopol to an alliance that the Russian leadership sees as an adversary. The U.S. would have faced a damnable dilemma. Either we would have sent American troops to fight for Ukraine at the price of Americans killing and being killed by Russians—with the risk that direct combat between the U.S. and Russia could escalate, even to a nuclear war. Or, we would have declined to come to Ukraine's defense with the result that U.S. security guarantees that provide the backbone for order both in Europe and in East Asia would be sharply devalued.

In 2008, the Russian-Georgian war raised a similar specter. Again, the good news was that Georgia had not been admitted to NATO. Nonetheless, as Angela Stent's *Limits of Partnership* documents, at an August 2008 principals meeting after members of Vice President Dick Cheney's staff had suggested a limited U.S. military response in support of Georgia, National Security Advisor Steve Hadley posed the question, "Are we prepared to go to war with Russia over Georgia?" When he went around the table to allow each member to answer the question, no one was prepared to say yes. As Hadley is quoted, "I wanted to make people show their cards about a possible military response."

Reflection on the challenge posed to the U.S. in the case of Russia's wars with Georgia and Ukraine underlines the central argument of this essay. American leaders, Democrats and Republicans alike, understand that America's most vital interest is the survival of the United States. To quote the mantra once more: to preserve the U.S. as a free nation with our fundamental institutions and values intact. As the only nation that can by its unilateral choice destroy the United States, Russia has a unique claim on American presidents' attention and priority. In Ronald Reagan's oft-repeated one-liner: a nuclear war can never be won and therefore never be fought.

That fact creates an inescapable bond between the U.S. and Russia: a vital shared interest in avoiding the nuclear war in which both would become the first victims.

In the Cuban Missile Crisis of 1962, President John F. Kennedy confronted Soviet leader Nikita Khrushchev "eyeball to eyeball" in a crisis Kennedy believed had one chance in three of ending in nuclear war. From this, JFK drew one central lesson: in relations between nuclear superpowers, each must avoid confrontations that force the adversary to choose between humiliating retreat and nuclear war. That reality has constrained American willingness to use combat forces in response to Russian challenges to anything other than vital American national interests.

Thus after having encouraged the Hungarian uprising of 1956, when Soviet troops invaded and crushed freedom fighters, President Dwight Eisenhower refused to come to their defense. When Czechoslovakia sought to throw off the Soviet shackles in 1968, President Lyndon Johnson chose not to send Americans to fight on their behalf. In Georgia in 2008 and Ukraine in 2014, Presidents Bush and Obama came to similar conclusions.

This issue is obviously much more complex than this brief summary. Elsewhere I have written about what I labeled the "nuclear paradox." In a world of mutual assured destruction (in which each nation can after being struck first retaliate in a way that destroys the other), while neither adversary can win a nuclear war, each must be willing to risk losing such a war.[9] The paradox arises from the juxtaposition of two hard truths. On the one hand, if through whatever combination of circumstances, nuclear war happens, both nations are destroyed. There is no value for which national leaders could rationally choose a war that destroys the U.S. In that sense, in the Cuban Missile Crisis, Kennedy and Khrushchev found themselves, in effect, partners in preventing mutual disaster.

On the other hand, leaders of both nations understand that reality—and know that their opponent does too. If one of the parties is so fearful of the consequences that it is unwilling to risk war, its adversary can force it to back down in any confrontation by threatening to take the dispute to that level. Thus to preserve the U.S. as a free nation with its fundamental institutions and values, American leaders must be willing not to choose war with the Soviet Union or Russia, but nonetheless to choose actions that increase the risk that this could be the outcome.

In response to Russia's aggression against Ukraine, an array of claims about impacts on U.S. and international interests have been asserted. These include:

- Russian-supported rebellion/war has *killed more than 3,600 people.*

- Russian annexation of Crimea undermines the post-Cold War order (NATO's then-Secretary General Anders Fogh Rasmussen: "the Post-Cold War order is at stake.").

- Russian use of military force to change borders in Europe threatens the *post-World War II international order* (Senator Marco Rubio: "Direct challenge and threat to post-World War II international order for which the United States and our allies have made great sacrifices over the past seven decades.").

- Russian actions in Crimea and eastern Ukraine *undermine the Free World* (Ukrainian President Petro Poroshenko: "Today's war will determine whether we will be forced to accept the reality of a dark-torn and bitter Europe as part of a new world order. ... It is a war for a Free World!").

- Russian actions in Crimea and eastern Ukraine are the *beginning of World War III* (Ukrainian Prime Minister Arseniy Yatsenyuk: "The world has not yet forgotten World War II, but Russia is already keen on starting World War III.").

- This is a *Munich moment* (British Prime Minister David Cameron: "We are running the risk of repeating the mistakes made in Munich in 1938.").

- Putin's actions are a bolt of lightning that illuminates for us his real ambition to *overturn the international order*—requiring a determined response aimed at *changing the regime* of Putin's Russia (*Washington Post* editorial: "The West should not shrink from destabilization of Mr. Putin's regime. The Kremlin ruler has evolved into a dangerous rogue who threatens the stability and peace of Europe.").

- Annexation of Crimea violates the *Budapest Memorandum* of 1994 in which the U.S. and Russia joined in committing themselves to respect Ukraine's sovereignty and territorial integrity as part of the package that persuaded Ukraine to eliminate what could have become the third largest nuclear arsenal in the world. A weak response in this case would devalue future credibility of analogous commitments to prevent proliferation of nuclear weapons.

Some of these are clearly correct; most appear to me highly unlikely. Nonetheless, in the case of two of the claims, the combination of likelihood and consequences require serious attention.

Assertions that Putin has a master plan to reestablish the former Soviet Union with or without the Warsaw Pact seem implausible. But historically we know that appetite can grow with eating. Were Putin to pay little or no costs for his annexation of Crimea and destabilization of eastern Ukraine, it is not unreasonable to worry that he might be tempted by other opportunities. In the former Soviet space, a number of countries like Kazakhstan have a substantial ethnic Russian population. These governments recognize that they must accord Russia a degree of deference and avoid what Russia would see as provocations, like seeking NATO membership.

More dangerous from the perspective of U.S. interests are the Baltic countries of Latvia, Estonia, and Lithuania that were admitted to NATO in 2004. If in response to Putin's annexation of Crimea, and the justification that he has offered for that action in the "Putin Doctrine," the U.S. and NATO were to fail to respond, it is conceivable that Putin, or some of his advisors, could imagine that he could replicate in Latvia a version of his not-so-stealthy invasion that seized Crimea. Recognizing that threat, the U.S. has moved to vivify a red line separating members of NATO from other states that may be friends or partners. It has also begun to operationalize that red line by rotating U.S. and other NATO forces regularly through the Baltic so that any Russian invasion of Latvia or the other Baltic states would unavoidably confront NATO troops. The Baltic countries, as well as other Europeans, could increase their security even further by becoming serious about their own defense capabilities, creating forces capable of denying Russia a quick or easy victory. If before invading Ukraine, Putin had believed he would face the equivalent of Afghanistan in 1979, or even Switzerland when German generals contemplated invading it during World War II, he might have come to a different conclusion.

The U.S. should never forget that as part of the process that persuaded Ukraine to eliminate its nuclear arsenal, the U.S. undertook obligations. In the Budapest Memorandum of 1994, the U.S., Russia, and the UK pledged to respect the sovereignty and territorial integrity of Ukraine. In annexing Crimea, Russia unambiguously violated that commitment. The U.S. did not commit itself to fight for Ukraine's territorial integrity, but it did make a commitment to consult and assist Ukraine. What we do at this point, and fail to do, to make Russia pay for violating this commitment will have consequences for the credibility of U.S. commitments in nonproliferation going forward.

Margins for impact are a function of level of effort. Even if Ukraine does not engage vital American national interests, and thus does not require that we fight for its defense, this does not mean that events there have no impact on American national interests, or that there is nothing we should do to make Putin's aggression costly for Russia. The U.S. and Europe have many sticks that can be applied, and many carrots that can be denied, short of sending combat boots on the ground. The current sectoral sanctions are damaging Russia's economy in the short run and, unless relieved, will have a much larger impact over the longer run. When Russia invaded Afghanistan in 1979, the CIA supported the Mujahidin opposition in an insurgency that after a decade of fighting led the Soviet Army to withdraw. Indeed, if the West really wanted to make Putin and his coterie regret the decision to destabilize eastern Ukraine, it could mobilize a combination of economic assistance, advice, and economic relations with Kiev that would give Ukraine a fighting chance to become a successful European country.

Given the bill for such an effort, and the odds of success, it remains to be seen whether Europeans and Americans will conclude that their national interests justify a Marshall Plan-level program of economic support for Ukraine. My bet is that the West's response in the economic arena will mirror that on the military battlefield and that in the months ahead, Ukraine's economic crisis will become the focus of attention, overshadowing the military conflict.

Part IV: The Obama administration's response

In assessing the Obama administration's performance in dealing with the Ukrainian crisis, it is useful to distinguish among three phases: crisis prevention, crisis management, and longer-term posture.

Preventive diplomacy could have achieved a "good enough" resolution of the issues prior to the 2013 wrestling match between the EU and Putin that led to the overthrow of Yanukovych and the current crisis. My scorecard gives low marks to the Obama administration, the Bush administration before it, and indeed the analytic community. If from a simple national-interest point of view one had asked how Putin's Russia was likely to react to the prospect of Ukraine joining NATO—and therefore effectively losing its Sevastopol naval base—his response was not unlikely. Prior to the crisis, it should not have been difficult for imaginative diplomats from the U.S., Russia, Ukraine, and the EU to agree on a European security framework for respecting sovereignty and territorial integrity, embodying Ukraine's commitment in its original declaration of independence of 1990 to be a "permanently neutral state that does not participate in military blocs."[10]

Once the EU, U.S., and Russia begin bidding for the Ukrainian government's allegiance and attempting to manipulate domestic politics in Ukraine (including Assistant Secretary Victoria Nuland's infamous "&*#! the EU!" contribution), my scorecard gives the administration low marks. U.S. policymakers showed little understanding of the dynamics and drivers of events inside Ukraine. U.S. public pronouncements were credible primarily to domestic constituents and post-modern Europeans.

Finally, on the big picture of the U.S. response to the Ukrainian crisis, I give the administration high marks to this point, October 2014:

- For recognizing that Russia's actions pose a serious threat, but not to vital American interests;

- For avoiding ownership of a problem that will get worse before it gets worse (and likely require one bailout after another);

- For not letting Putin use this issue to drive a wedge between Europe and the U.S. but, in fact, with unexpected leadership from Chancellor Merkel, fashioning a coordinated response;

- For resisting political pressure to fall back to Cold War II while keeping open the possibility of an ugly but acceptable outcome that allows cooperation with Putin in select arenas, especially on Iran; and

- For not following the advice of the individual who would have been president had he defeated Obama in 2008, and his senatorial colleagues like Lindsay Graham, former Senator Joe Lieberman, the *Washington Post* editorial page, and former UN Ambassador John Bolton, to send arms and advisors to Ukraine or to take Putin's provocation as an opportunity to admit Ukraine to NATO now.[11]

Graham Allison is Director of the Belfer Center for Science and International Affairs and Douglas Dillon Professor of Government at Harvard's John F. Kennedy School of Government. As "Founding Dean" of the Kennedy School, under his leadership, from 1977 to 1989, a small, undefined program grew twenty-fold to become a major professional school of public policy and government. Dr. Allison has served as Special Advisor to the Secretary of Defense under President Reagan and as Assistant Secretary of Defense for Policy and Plans under President Clinton, where he coordinated DOD strategy and policy towards Russia, Ukraine, and the other states of the former Soviet Union. He has the sole distinction of having twice been awarded the Department of Defense's highest civilian award, the Distinguished Public Service Medal, first by Secretary Cap Weinberger and second by Secretary Bill Perry. He served as a member of the Defense Policy Board for Secretaries Weinberger, Carlucci, Cheney, Aspin, Perry, and Cohen. His first book, *Essence of Decision: Explaining the Cuban Missile Crisis* (1971), was released in a revised second edition (1999) and ranks among the all-time bestsellers with more than 450,000 copies in print. His latest book (2013), *Lee Kuan Yew: The Grand Master's Insights on China, the United States and the World* (co-authored with Robert Blackwill), has been a bestseller in the U.S. and abroad. His previous book, *Nuclear Terrorism: The Ultimate Preventable Catastrophe*, was selected by *The New York Times* as one of the "100 most notable books of 2004." He is a member of the Aspen Strategy Group.

[1] See: Ellsworth, Robert, Andrew Goodpaster, and Rita Hauser, Co-chairs. July 2000. *America's National Interests: A Report from The Commission on America's National Interests, 2000*. Washington, DC: Report for Commission on America's National Interests.

The Commission report does note, however, that war between Russia and Ukraine would impact extremely important American interests.

[2] Many colleagues will object. It is often argued that since Ukraine is a sovereign country, it cannot be denied the right to choose whatever security arrangements (including NATO membership) it believes best serves its interests. While correct, the U.S. and its NATO partners are also sovereign countries that have equivalent rights to choose whatever security arrangements serve their interests. And my view is that these interests are best served by stating clearly that in current and foreseeable geopolitical realities, Ukrainian membership in NATO is not an option. Diplomatically, this can be explained in terms of the guideline on unresolved territorial conflicts in NATO's Membership Action Plan, subhead 1.2.C, that states "aspirants would also be expected to settle ethnic disputes or external territorial disputes including irredentist claims or internal jurisdictional disputes by peaceful means in accordance with OSCE principles." This functions as a precondition for candidacy in NATO and has been applied in the case of Azerbaijan, Armenia, Serbia, and Georgia.

[3] In game theory, these are "mixed-motive" or "interdependent" games that as Thomas Schelling explains are defined by "ambivalence in relation to the other player—the mixture of mutual dependence and conflict, of partnership and competition." Schelling, Thomas. 1960. *Strategy of Conflict*. Cambridge, MA: Harvard University Press. p. 89.

[4] Allison, Graham. 2000. "Russia's Domestic Political Future and U.S. National Interests." Chapter in *America and Russia: Memos to a President*, Robert Zoellick and Phillip Zelikow, Eds. New York, NY: W.W. Norton & Company.

[5] Allison, Graham, Robert D. Blackwill, Dimitri K. Simes, and Paul J. Saunders. October 2011. *Russia and U.S. National Interests: Why Should Americans Care?* Washington, D.C. and Cambridge, MA: Center for the National Interest and Belfer Center for Science and International Affairs, Harvard Kennedy School.

[6] In the case of Ukraine, such a test might ask: In the past millennium, Ukraine has been an independent state for X years? Historically, before Khrushchev transferred Crimea to Ukraine in 1954, in which centuries had Crimea been part of Ukraine? Having started in 1991(when the Soviet Union imploded), with a per capita GDP equal to Belarus, Ukraine's per capita GDP is now Y that of Belarus? Geographically, Ukraine shares borders with Z states? In eastern Ukraine, V% of the population identify themselves as ethnic Russians. In the next three years, Ukrainian repayments of debts due to the external creditors = X?

[7] This partial list serves only as a reminder. Having little understanding of Ukraine, when combined with my small-c (Burkean) conservatism, this leaves me cautious about social engineering and reserved about prescribing interventions.

[8] Allison, Graham. March 21, 2014. "Good News from Ukraine: It Doesn't Have Nukes," *National Interest*.

[9] Allison, Graham, and Richard E. Neustadt. 1971. "Afterword" in *Thirteen Days: A Memoir of the Cuban Missile Crisis*. New York, NY: W.W. Norton & Company.

[10] See, for example, Nunn, Sam, Wolfgang Ischinger, and Igor Ivanov, Co-chairs. February 2012. *Toward a Euro-Atlantic Security Community*, EASI Final Report. Moscow, Russia; Brussels, Belgium; and Washington, DC: Carnegie Endowment for International Peace.

[11] "NATO membership for Ukraine undoubtedly carries risks, but no alternative can provide anything like the necessary security to stop further Russian interference. Had the Europeans backed Bush in 2008, we might well have deterred Russian military aggression in both Georgia and Ukraine." Bolton, John. May 5, 2014. *Weekly Standard*.

"[T]he first priority is to help Ukraine succeed...Putin and the Russian government have picked Ukraine as the central battleground in their struggle against "the West." They win if the Ukrainian economy fails, which means that the United States and Europe win only if the Ukrainian economy succeeds."

—STEPHEN HADLEY

Concluding Observations:
What We Heard

Stephen Hadley
Principal
RiceHadleyGates, LLC

In this chapter, I will try to draw together the four days of discussion at the 2014 Aspen Strategy Group Summer Workshop, titled "Redux: Prescriptions for U.S.-Russia Relations." Let me thank in advance those workshop participants whose comments I have incorporated into this essay. Though the agreed-upon rules of the workshop preclude me from citing them by name, I will start by using the analytical framework that Graham Allison offered in his very good chapter presented at the workshop and found in this book.

For four days, we discussed what is happening with Russia, Ukraine, and the United States and what to do about it. Why should the United States care about what is happening between Russia and Ukraine? The United States should care because it threatens the Europe "whole, free, and at peace" that is a core U.S. national interest. Given the challenges the United States faces, not having that kind of Europe as a U.S. partner puts at risk America's future "as a free nation with its fundamental institutions and values intact"—Graham's definition of a vital U.S. national interest.

What is the U.S. margin of impact on the Russia-Ukraine situation? The U.S. impact on the situation may be limited but when combined with that of Europe, it is not. U.S. and EU collective military, economic, and diplomatic strength—and the strength of their shared values—dwarf the strength of Russia and give the United States and Europe together great margin of impact if they are willing to use it and wise enough to use it effectively.

So the first thing for the United States to do is develop a common strategy on Ukraine and Russia with Europe. The Europeans have the leverage—positive and negative—due to their greater trade and investment and economic and energy interdependence with Russia. And it is the European businesses, economies, and popular well-being that will be most directly affected by the strategy that Europe and the United States adopt. Developing a common strategy will require an intensive effort: not just periodic 30-minute phone calls or 1½-hour fly-in, fly-out meetings.

In developing a common U.S.-European strategy, what is the first thing that needs to be done? Establish the objectives of that strategy. As one workshop participant so aptly said, what is lost in any meeting of more than two government officials is any sense of what they are trying to accomplish! The United States and Europe need to clarify objectives before they can develop a strategy to achieve those objectives. The objective should be a Europe "whole, free, and at peace"—and I would add "in which Russia finds its peaceful place."

What does this objective for Europe mean for our objective for Russia? Drawing from Steve Biegun's paper (also a chapter in this book) and our discussion, the objective should be for a stable, democratic Russia at peace with its neighbors, integrated into the European economic system and the global economy and working with the United States and Europe to address global challenges.

What is a strategy for Russia that seeks to achieve this objective? This is a big effort to which I cannot do justice here. Russia is at a tipping point: it is trending away from the objective described above—becoming more authoritarian, less free at home, more aggressive abroad, and moving away from economic integration with Europe and the global economy. So there is some urgency in coming up with an effective strategy. Such a strategy will have short-term and long-term aspects.

Short term

The United States and Europe need to make a strategic choice: Should they give up on Putin? Look past him? Isolate him internationally? Seek to destabilize him and his regime—a "regime change" policy? Many Russians think that is precisely U.S. policy. But it is not U.S. policy, as I understand it, and it should not be U.S. policy.

The objective should be to change the direction of Russian policy, not try to change the Russian regime—which the United States and Europe could not do and would hurt their interests if they tried. A short-term strategy to achieve this objective should include the following elements:

1. Don't demonize Putin—it plays into his grievance narrative and makes him into a domestic hero within Russia.

2. Try to construct reliable channels to Putin—from Europe and from the United States. From the United States, candidates include Stanley Fisher (especially

where sanctions are concerned) and James A. Baker III (especially if it comes to trying to broker a solution to the Ukrainian crisis). From Europe, Angela Merkel is probably the best candidate.

3. Listen to Putin, try to understand what he is saying, and show him respect even while standing up firmly against policies that threaten American and European interests.

4. Use Putin's dislike for international isolation as an incentive for good behavior (while avoiding systematic, across-the-board isolation that could provoke an extreme reaction).

5. Show clear respect for Russia and the Russian people; make a distinction between them and the Russian government—making clear that it is the policies of the Russian government to which the United States and Europe object.

6. Do not reject Russia or seek to sever its historical and economic ties to the rest of Europe, but leave the door open for improved relations with Russia—and further economic integration of Russia with Europe and the global economy—once the Russian government turns away from current counterproductive policies.

7. Confront bad behavior and actions contrary to American and European interests; seek to frustrate and defeat the Russian government's misadventures abroad that threaten those interests.

8. Show strength in U.S. and EU foreign policy and avoid weakness—without strength and firmness, neither Putin nor the Russian people will respect either Europe or the United States.

9. Counter the Russian government's propaganda narrative with the truth—never let a falsehood go unchallenged—and expose publicly to international and Russian audiences what the Russian government is doing to destabilize its neighbors abroad and increasingly oppress the Russian people at home.

10. Develop and put in place the "full tool set" of positive and negative incentives that seek to move the Russian government toward the U.S. and European objective for Russia.

11. Generally, the United States and the EU should say what they will do in response to a challenge or crisis and then do what they say—less rhetoric, more action.

12. Continue and expand cooperation in areas where the United States and the EU share common interests with the Russian government; try to develop a robust agenda of cooperative projects in these areas.

13. The United States and the EU can both confront the actions of Putin and the Russian government that threaten their interests and still pursue a robust agenda of cooperation with the Russian government in such existing areas of cooperation as countering terrorism, stopping the proliferation of weapons of mass destruction (WMD), avoiding pandemic diseases, ensuring adequate and secure energy resources for the world economy, and dealing with environmental damage. These are all in the interest of the Russian government and the Russian people.

The Russian government's cooperation in these areas is not a favor to the United States and Europe. Cutting off this cooperation will only hurt Russia and the Russian people. Even if it decides to cut these ties, at some point the Russian government will change its mind and resume such cooperation—for its own interests.

Similarly, the fact that both the Russian and the American governments have nuclear weapons capable of destroying each other should not deter the United States from confronting Russian actions that threaten U.S. interests. One of the benefits of the end of the Cold War is that the risk of nuclear war has been dramatically reduced if not eliminated for both sides. Any residual nuclear risk has not deterred Putin from confronting the United States and the EU in Ukraine—it should not deter us from pushing back in a smart way.

Long term

Here again, the United States and Europe need to make a strategic choice. As one expert's presentation showed, Russia faces severe economic, demographic, educational, and social challenges, vulnerabilities, and weaknesses that suggest to some a nation in decline. Should the United States and Europe seek to exploit these problems? Or as another contributor framed the issue, should they seek to encourage a fast Russian decline or a slow Russian decline—or should they seek to work with Russia to reverse this projected decline?

Still another pointed out that this situation could be truly dangerous: rarely in history has a major nation state with great military power been so disinvested in the international system and had such dim prospects. The best course for the United

States and Europe may be to stand ready to work with the Russian government to reverse this projected decline once Russian leaders emerge who are open to such cooperation. A long-term strategy to achieve this objective should include the following elements:

1. Some in the group argued persuasively for direct support to progressive elements within Russian society that share U.S. and EU objectives for Russia: non-governmental organizations (NGOs), dissidents, human rights activists, democratic political elements and organizations, and the like. There is, of course, great risk that any hint of outside "Western" support will discredit these elements with the Russian population and subject them to great risk of physical harm. This is exactly what has happened to NGOs receiving funds from abroad—they have been forced to register as "foreign agents," the kiss of death within Russian society. The U.S. government and the EU must tread very carefully here.

2. Most everyone in the group seemed to agree on the need for a vigorous and robust information campaign to counter Russian government propaganda. As one speaker pointed out, such a campaign not only rebuts propaganda and falsehood with the truth but also makes it harder for the Russian propagandists to sustain their lies. Needed are multiple vehicles for spreading truth about and inside Russia and exposing the government's outrages—political crackdowns, corruption, self-dealing, human rights abuses, and destruction of any institutions not controlled by the Kremlin. While there is clearly a role for government here, European efforts may meet less resistance (and run less risk of being counterproductive) than U.S. efforts—and non-governmental initiatives may be more useful than those of governments.

3. There was strong support within the group for indirect assistance to those elements within Russian society that over the long term are more likely to move it in the direction of the U.S. and EU objectives for Russia. This would include measures to encourage private businesses, entrepreneurs, and consuming classes—constituencies that over the long term will be natural supporters of the rule of law, transparency, and more democratic institutions. To encourage these groups, the United States and the EU should encourage and incentivize the resumed and continued integration of Russia into the European and global economies.

4. Finally, our group widely supported expanded people-to-people exchanges wherever possible, at all levels in society, and particularly with Russians outside of traditional elites—as Steve Biegun says in his chapter, Russians who would rather work than march.

But this U.S.-EU strategy for Russia will be stillborn if a solution cannot be found to the Ukrainian crisis. This is not just because the Ukraine issue is the most important—and most urgent—issue on the current U.S.-Russia agenda. It is because if the Russian government succeeds in eastern Ukraine, it is likely to try to repeat its destabilization and subversion strategy elsewhere—perhaps on a NATO member state like Latvia. If it does, then it risks war with the United States and Europe under NATO's Article 5 guarantee to Latvia. A war in Europe would be a disaster for everyone.

Moreover, a Russian government success in Ukraine will take Russia further and further away from the U.S.-EU objective for Russia—perhaps decisively so. In its starkest terms, the United States and Europe cannot achieve a Europe "whole, free, and at peace in which Russia finds its peaceful place" if Putin succeeds in Ukraine.

What should be the U.S.-European objective for Ukraine? Ukraine should be a sovereign, independent, successful state at peace with its neighbors and its own citizens and free of outside interference. What is a strategy to achieve this objective? If one looks at what the U.S. government is actually doing with respect to the Ukraine crisis—and not just at what it is saying—current U.S. strategy appears largely to be sanctioning Russia until it "butts out" of Ukraine and stops its destabilization and subversion campaign.

If that is the essence of American policy, then there are a number of problems. First, it risks failure. Because of business opposition and divisions among EU nations, the simple fact is that the United States and the EU are unlikely to be able to impose heavy enough sanctions to persuade Putin to abandon his project in Ukraine. Second, it is inconsistent with the broader U.S.-EU objective for Russia. Sanctions only add to the already serious problems burdening the Russian economy and encourage its de-integration from the broader European and global economies. Third, it plays into Putin's "Russia as victim" narrative and, in the short run, strengthens his hold on Russia.

A better strategy is one that supplements current sanctions with more focus on other underutilized elements of strategy that are likely to have a greater impact on Putin and Russian government policy over the longer term. Of these, the first priority is to help Ukraine succeed. As one ASG member pointed out, Putin and the Russian government have picked Ukraine as the central battleground in their struggle against "the West." They win if the Ukrainian economy fails, which means that the United States and Europe win only if the Ukrainian economy succeeds.

Our group was almost unanimous about the need for a robust economic strategy for Ukraine with lots of external support—even as some members of the group expressed real doubts as to whether any such effort could succeed given Congressional reluctance to fund it and the many tools that the Russian government has to thwart it. One participant made the point that technical assistance was as important as financial help for the Ukrainian government and not just from governments but from the private sector and the Ukrainian expat community as well.

An effort should be made to convince the Russian government that Ukraine's economic success will not come at Russia's expense and to do so by preserving the traditional economic ties between Ukraine and Russia—arguing for a win-win rather than zero-sum approach. Indeed, an effort should be made to persuade the Russian government to join with the International Monetary Fund, World Bank, the EU, and the United States in a joint effort to reform and restore the Ukrainian economy—an effort that would not only ultimately benefit the Russian economy but would also help restore Russia's badly frayed standing among the Ukrainian people.

The group largely supported U.S. and EU efforts to support the Ukrainian security forces in their struggle against the Russian-backed separatists. Almost everyone in the group seemed to favor providing non-lethal assistance, and many favored training and equipping Ukrainian security forces with lethal arms. The goal here is to try to seek an end to Putin's destabilization and subversion campaign without producing another "frozen conflict"—with Putin using a territorial dispute between Russia and Ukraine to seek to discourage Ukraine's further movement toward the West and the EU and NATO from moving Ukraine toward membership.

The group discussed the prospects of a diplomatic settlement to the Ukrainian issue along the following lines: while Putin cannot afford for domestic political reasons to be seen as abandoning the Russia-backed separatists in eastern Ukraine, if Ukrainian forces can bring them to the brink of defeat, then Putin may opt for a face-saving diplomatic settlement as an alternative to open warfare with Ukraine. Ukrainian President Poroshenko cannot afford to show weakness, to surrender Ukrainian territory, or to accept Russian mercenaries on Ukrainian soil but could strengthen his domestic political standing if he is seen as having settled the conflict with Russia on terms that preserve these redlines.

A special envoy from the United States (such as the aforementioned James A. Baker III) or from the EU (such as German Chancellor Merkel or former German Ambassador to the United States Wolfgang Ischinger) or better yet both—working in tandem to reinforce U.S.-EU unity—could be involved behind the scenes in helping to arrange the deal. But it must be seen as Poroshenko's initiative since he will need this diplomatic success to give him the added political clout he will need domestically to sell the Ukrainian people on the difficult economic reforms that are required to restore the Ukrainian economy. The terms of the deal could include:

1. Extensive political and economic autonomy to eastern Ukraine to manage its own affairs but without veto power over Kiev's decisions on matters of national foreign and domestic policy;

2. Preservation of Ukraine's traditional economic ties with Russia without prejudice to Ukraine's increased ties to the EU (with agreed measures ensuring that such increased ties do not unfairly prejudice Ukrainian economic activity with Russia);

3. Return to Russia of all Russian mercenaries and other Russian citizens who came from Russia into Ukraine to participate in the insurrection;

4. Restoration of Ukrainian governmental control over all border crossing points into Russia;

5. Amnesty and the right to participate in Ukrainian political life for all those Ukrainians who participated in the insurrection (and who do not have blood on their hands) but are willing to put down their arms and pledge allegiance to the Ukrainian government in Kiev;

6. Inclusion of provisions protecting the political, economic, ethnic, and cultural (including linguistic) rights of all Ukrainian citizens;

7. Incorporation of the Poroshenko statement that Ukraine has no intention of seeking NATO membership for the duration of his term in office (with some in our group favoring an absolute bar to Ukrainian membership in NATO and others opposing such a firm bar so as not to reward Putin's bad behavior with respect to Ukraine); and

8. Some formulation that leaves the status of Crimea as an issue but does not seek to resolve it in this agreement. It was suggested that the U.S. government has developed in detail a potential diplomatic settlement along these lines but that, so far at least, the Russian government has expressed no interest in a deal.

Other elements of a strategy to help resolve the Ukrainian conflict and reduce the risk of its repetition elsewhere include steps that seek to:

1. Deter further Russian government intervention in Ukraine or elsewhere. The United States should recommit to the security of Europe through additional U.S. military deployments and U.S. military exercises at the eastern frontiers of NATO Europe in the Baltics, Poland, and the Balkans. NATO should revitalize itself through additional planning, exercises, and military capabilities for the core mission of security in Europe with emphasis on defending the eastern frontiers of NATO. The United States and the EU should work together with NATO to help nations potentially subject to Russian pressure strengthen their capacity to defend their territories from either armed attack or subversion— not with the expectation of defeating Russian military forces but increasing the costs to Russia of such intervention and thereby helping to deter intervention in the first place. These same steps will also reassure NATO allies vulnerable to pressure from Russia that NATO stands by its Article 5 guarantee of their security.

2. Deny Putin targets of opportunity by eliminating or hardening Europe's vulnerabilities and divisions against his opportunistic exploitation. Some examples include:

   - Complete the Transatlantic Trade and Investment Partnership (TTIP) binding Europe and the United States in a relationship of economic growth and prosperity, leaving the door open to adding participants such as Turkey and, ultimately, a peaceful and democratic Russia.

   - Develop a joint transatlantic energy strategy using liquid natural gas shipments from the United States, shale oil and shale gas produced in Europe, creative use of existing pipeline infrastructure, and construction of new non-Russian-controlled pipelines to reduce Europe's dependence on Russian-origin oil and gas.

   - Resume the EU's "open door" policy of offering association agreements and, ultimately, membership to countries to the east that seek them (with arrangements that do not require severing historical and economic ties to Russia).

- Reenergize the U.S.-EU vision of a Europe "whole, free, and at peace in which Russia finds its peaceful place" as an alternative to Putin's vision of Russian domination of its neighbors and increasing authoritarianism at home.

Stephen Hadley is a principal of RiceHadleyGates LLC, an international strategic consulting firm founded with Condoleezza Rice, Robert Gates, and Anja Manuel. RiceHadleyGates assists senior executives of major corporations in overcoming the challenges to doing business successfully in major emerging markets like China, India, Brazil, Turkey, and Indonesia. Mr. Hadley is also Board Chairman of the United States Institute of Peace (USIP). He has co-chaired a series of senior bipartisan working groups on topics such as Arab-Israeli peace, U.S. political strategy in Afghanistan and Pakistan, U.S./Turkey relations, and U.S. policy on Iraq and Egypt. Mr. Hadley served for four years as the Assistant to the President for National Security Affairs from 2005-2009. In that capacity he was the principal White House foreign policy advisor to then President George W. Bush, directed the National Security Council staff, and ran the interagency national security policy development and execution process. From 2001 to 2005, he was the Assistant to the President and Deputy National Security Advisor, serving under then National Security Advisor Condoleezza Rice. In addition to covering the full range of national security issues, Mr. Hadley had special responsibilities in several areas, including a U.S./Russia political dialogue, the Israeli disengagement from Gaza, and developing a strategic relationship with India. He is a member of the Aspen Strategy Group.